V₂<1

S0-AVZ-606

NICARAGUA

PROFILES • NATIONS OF CONTEMPORARY LATIN AMERICA
Ronald Schneider, Series Editor

NICARAGUA

The Land of Sandino

Thomas W. Walker

Westview Press / Boulder, Colorado

Nations of Contemporary Latin America

The drawing on the jacket and paperback cover, entitled *Amanecer en Nicaragua* (Awakening in Nicaragua), was drawn especially for this book by Leoncio Sáenz of Managua. An artist of considerable acclaim in Central America, Sáenz is a frequent artistic contributor to *Nicaráuac*, a monthly publication of the Nicaraguan Ministry of Culture.

Second printing, 1982

Published in 1981 in the United States of America by
  Westview Press, Inc.
  5500 Central Avenue
  Boulder, Colorado 80301
  Frederick A. Praeger, Publisher

Library of Congress Cataloging in Publication Data
Walker, Thomas W.
  Nicaragua: the land of Sandino.
  (Nations of contemporary Latin America)
  Bibliography: p.
  Includes index.
  1. Nicaragua – History.   I. Title.   II. Series.
F1526.W175   972.85   81-11418
ISBN 0-89158-940-6   AACR2
ISBN 0-86531-273-7 (pbk.)

Printed and bound in the United States of America

To the Proud and Indomitable People of Nicaragua,
with Profound Respect and Love

Contents

Illustrations

Foreword

For many countries of Latin America, as well as for much of the rest of the so-called Third World, dependency is a basic fact of life. Related to, yet differentiated from the elemental Marxist concept of imperialism, dependency theory in recent years has evolved into a framework for analyzing the political dilemmas and developmental processes of such countries. It has proved most useful when applied to frustrated or even abortive experiences with modernization, especially those cases in which the most intractable problems are rooted in a peripheral relationship to the international economic system and subordination to one of the world's superpowers in the political realm. Since this has been the fundamental situation of Nicaragua until very recently, a modified dependency perspective is highly appropriate for Professor Walker's insightful study of this troubled Central American nation.

Nicaragua, with its long history of dictatorships and foreign intervention, followed by a dramatic revolution at the end of the 1970s, is certainly a most timely choice for the first volume in the *Nations of Contemporary Latin America* series. Here the United States, once it replaced Great Britain as the Western Hemisphere paramount (around the turn of the century), exercised an all but suffocating influence – one which produced both the Somoza dynasty and the Sandinist revolutionaries. Significantly, the confrontation between the original protagonists in this prolonged drama, Augusto César Sandino and Anastasio Somoza García, occurred during the early years of Franklin D. Roosevelt's "Good Neighbor Policy" when the United States was beginning to pull back from its most heavy-handed direct domination of Latin America. It would take nearly a half century for the political heirs of the martyred Sandino to topple the *Somocista* system erected during the 1930s, and great questions concerning the essential nature of the post-revolutionary regime remain to be resolved in the 1980s.

This book, like its sister studies in the series that will employ other analytical approaches to countries whose essential problems are of a significantly different nature, does not attempt to predict the future course of events. Its author does, however, meet the challenge of presenting a coherent interpretation of Nicaraguan reality, which will make the controversial events of the coming years intelligible to those seeking answers along the way to the questions of why developments are following a certain course. This is a critical contribution at a point in time when the yet new administration in Washington appears strongly inclined to reassert the traditional U.S. voice and presence in the still fluid post-Somoza processes. Developments in and concerning Nicaragua during the early and mid-1980s will surely give rise to heated debate. This perceptive profile should provide needed focus and understanding to this debate and assure that at least some of the participants will be well informed on the serious issues involved.

Ronald Schneider

Acknowledgments

I would like to express my gratitude to a number of individuals, groups, and institutions who helped produce this book. First, thanks are due the Nicaraguan people and government for their kind hospitality and extensive cooperation. I am also indebted to the Department of Political Science, the College of Arts and Sciences, and the Office of Research and Sponsored Programs at Ohio University for the financial support that enabled me to make four trips to Nicaragua following the liberation. For kindly agreeing to read and comment on various segments of the manuscript, thanks are due Alejandro Bendaña, Ricardo Chavarria, Kenneth P. Erickson, Susan E. Ramírez-Horton, Charles Stansifer, Eric Wagner, Anne U. Walker, and Sergio Zeledón. I am also grateful to the editors of *Caribbean Review, Current History,* and Houghton Mifflin and Company for their kind permission to use occasional phrases, sentences, and paragraphs that appeared in earlier works of mine for which they hold the copyrights. The work of several efficient and dedicated typists is also gratefully acknowledged. Finally, my deep appreciation goes to my wife, Anne, and my children, Joe, Carlos, Jimmy, and Emilie, for understanding and support beyond the call of duty.

T.W.W.

Abbreviations

AMNLAE	Luisa Amanda Espinosa Association of Nicaraguan Women
AMPRONAC	Association of Women Confronting the National Problem
ANS	Sandinist Children's Association
ATC	The Rural Workers' Association
CDC	Civil Defense Committee
CDS	Sandinist Defense Committee
CONDECA	Central American Defense Council
COPPPAL	Permanent Conference of Political Parties of Latin America
COSEP	Superior Council of Private Enterprise
CST	Sandinist Workers' Central
EPS	Sandinist Popular Army
FAO	Broad Opposition Front
FIR	Nicaraguan International Reconstruction Fund
FSLN	Sandinist Front of National Liberation
INCAE	Central American Institute of Business Administration
INPRHU	Institute of Human Promotion
JGRN	Governing Junta of National Reconstruction
JS-19	19th of July Sandinist Youth
MINVAH	Ministry of Housing and Human Settlements

MPS	Sandinist Popular Militias
OAS	Organization of American States
PLI	Independent Liberal party
PPSC	Popular Social Christian party
PRI	Institutional Revolutionary party (Mexico)
PS	Sandinist Police
PSCN	Nicaraguan Social Christian party
PSN	Nicaraguan Socialist party

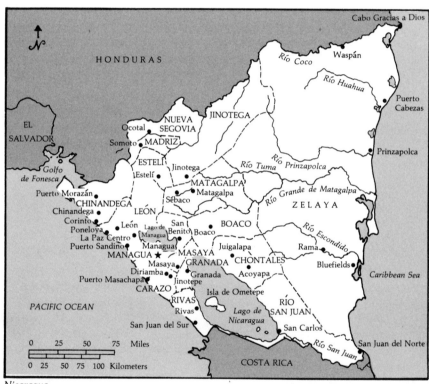

Nicaragua

1

Introduction

Located at the geographic center of Central America, with Honduras to the north and Costa Rica to the south, Nicaragua is the largest country in the region. Even so, its 57,143 square miles (148,000 square kilometers) of surface make it only slightly larger than the state of Iowa. Its population of about 2.5 million is slightly smaller than Iowa's 2.8 million. Nevertheless, Nicaragua is an extremely interesting and unique country with an importance that far exceeds its size. Although there have been many revolts and coups d'etat in Latin America, Nicaragua is one of only a handful of Latin American countries to have experienced a real social revolution, by which I mean a rapid process of change in social and economic as well as political structures.

The physical characteristics of Nicaragua have long drawn the attention and captured the imagination of outsiders. The country has abundant and rich agricultural lands, considerable potential for geothermal and hydroelectric energy, important timber and mineral resources, and conveniently located waterways that make Nicaragua an ideal site for an interoceanic canal.

Though located entirely within the tropics, this small country varies from one region to another in temperature and other climatic characteristics. Altitude, mountainous land barriers, and the differing meteorological influences of the Caribbean and Pacific oceans are the determining factors. As throughout the tropics, altitude rather than season determines temperature. On the lowlands of the Pacific and Caribbean coasts temperatures usually are quite high. In the central mountain ranges—or Cordilleras—that transverse the country from northwest to southeast, the climate is temperate. The mountains also influence Nicaraguan weather by acting as a natural barrier between the predominantly humid environment of the Caribbean and the seasonally dry patterns of the Pacific.

As a result of these factors, Nicaragua can be divided conceptu-

1

ally into three distinct regions: the Caribbean lowlands, the central highlands, and the western lowlands. Occupying nearly half of the country, the Caribbean lowlands are composed of hot, humid, tropical rain forests, swamps, and savannahs. As the most appropriate type of agricultural activity in such an environment involves the primitive technique of slash-and-burn, this vast region has never been able to support a large human population – at present less than 8 percent of the national total lives there.

Due to the more moderate and seasonal nature of rainfall in the central highlands and western lowlands, these regions are more inviting for commercial agriculture and human habitation. The temperate climate and rich soils of the highlands make an ideal environment for coffee cultivation. Indeed, some of the best coffee in the world comes from the highland department of Matagalpa. The western lowlands are appropriate for such crops as cotton, rice, and sugar. A chain of volcanos running through the western lowlands from northwest to southeast enriches the soil of the region through frequent dustings of volcanic ash. The principal cities and most of the population of Nicaragua are in the western lowlands.

Another important physical factor is the position of certain large lakes and rivers. Even in the colonial period, explorers and settlers knew that interoceanic travel across Nicaragua was possible via water routes, taking advantage of the San Juan River, Lake Nicaragua, and Lake Managua. The amount of overland travel required to complete the journey was small. As a result Nicaraguan waterways were regularly used as commercial routes for transisthmian travel during the nearly three centuries of colonial rule. And, in the nineteenth and twentieth centuries, the country's obvious potential as a canal site made Nicaragua the object of frequent foreign intrigue and intervention.

Nicaragua is blessed not only in natural resources and environment but also in certain demographic, social, and cultural characteristics. First, unlike some Latin American countries, it is not overpopulated. Indeed, although it has an abundance of arable land, Nicaragua's population is relatively small. Second, the people are relatively homogeneous and culturally integrated. There are no major racial, ethnic, linguistic, or religious divisions. Practically all Nicaraguans are Catholic, speak Spanish, and share a common cultural heritage. The majority are mestizo, a mixture of Spanish and Indian. And, though there are some "pure" whites, Indians, and blacks, little racial prejudice exists. Finally, Nicaraguans are a congenial, outgoing people with every reason to be proud of things *nica*, such as their distinctive cookery, music, dialect, literary heritage, and sense of humor.

Ironically, in spite of its human and natural potential, Nicaragua is a poor country and the majority of the people have endured great oppression throughout history. Even in the late 1970s the annual gross national product (GNP) per capita was only a little over $800 (U.S.). And this statistic obscures the fact that income in Nicaragua was so unevenly distributed that 50 percent of the people probably had an annual disposable income of only $200. This, in turn, means that the average citizen lived in inadequate housing, ate poorly, and, prior to the 1979 revolution, had little access to education, health care, or other public services. In 1979 the estimated life expectancy at birth for the average Nicaraguan was fifty-three years—ten years less than the average for Central America and eighteen years less than the average for the Latin American nation with the greatest longevity, Cuba.[1]

The roots of Nicaragua's problem lie in a phenomenon that many social scientists refer to as *dependency*. Most countries in the world are dependent to one degreee or another on other countries. Interdependence does not necessarily imply dependency. Dependency refers to a specific situation in which the economy of a weak country is externally oriented and the government is controlled by national and/or international elites or classes that benefit from this economic relationship. Whereas the dominant elites in an industrial country usually have an interest in maintaining a healthy society and, therefore, a citizenry capable of consuming at high levels, the rulers of a dependent society have no such interest because their markets are largely external. For them, the common citizen is important not as a potential consumer but rather as a source of cheap and easily exploitable labor. In such societies both the means of production and income tend increasingly to be concentrated in a few hands. Though impressive growth in the GNP often occurs, significant benefits almost never "trickle down" to the people, no matter how long the process goes on and no matter how much development takes place.[2]

Prerevolutionary Nicaragua was an extreme case of this common phenomenon. Since the days of the Spanish conquest in the sixteenth century, the Nicaraguan economy had always been externally oriented and the people who exercised power had been the beneficiaries of this relationship. First, hundreds of thousands of Indians were exported as slaves. Later, when that "resource" was used up, the elites exported timber, beef, and hides. During the late nineteenth century, coffee became an important product on the world

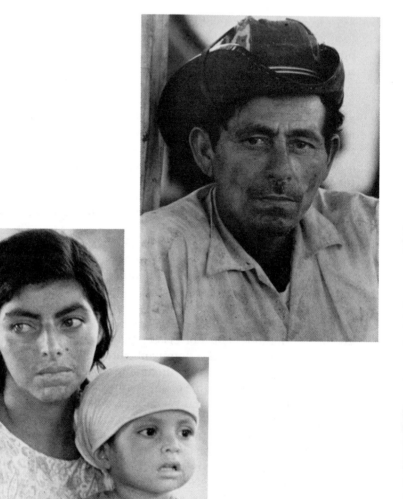

From left to right: Some Nicaraguans. Ranchhand; mother and child (photos courtesy of Harvey Williams). Boys with slingshot; market woman (photos courtesy of Alberto Mendez of the Center for Agrarian Education and Promotion, Managua).

market. In the twentieth century, especially after the Second World War, the country developed a diversified repertoire of exports ranging from cotton, coffee, and sugar to beef and gold. Throughout Nicaraguan history, a small elite controlled most of the means of production and garnered most of the benefits. The country's rulers – whether openly dictatorial or ostensibly democratic – always governed in behalf of the privileged few.

Paralleling this history of domestic exploitation – and frequently an essential ingredient of it – was a history of foreign intervention and control. During the colonial period, the Spanish faced sporadic challenges from the British government and English pirates for control of Nicaraguan territory. In the middle of the nineteenth century, the country was actually ruled by a U.S. citizen for a brief period. In the twentieth century, the U.S. government imposed its dominion over Nicaragua first by direct armed intervention (from 1912 to 1925 and from 1926 to 1933) and later through the client dictatorships of the Somoza family (from 1936 to 1979).

Yet if dependency, exploitation, and mass deprivation constitute recurrent themes in Nicaraguan history, so, too, do the ideas of nationalism and popular resistance. Nicaraguan history and folklore are replete with nationalist heroes and martyrs: the Indian *cacique* ("chief"), Diriangén, who fought against the Spanish at the outset of the colonial period; Andrés Castro, who took a stand against the forces of the North American filibuster-president, William Walker, in the mid-nineteenth century; the liberal dictator José Santos Zelaya, who defied British and U.S. imperial designs at the turn of the century; Benjamín Zeledón and Augusto César Sandino, who fought the U.S. occupiers in the early twentieth century; and Carlos Fonseca Amador, a cofounder of the Sandinist Front of National Liberation (FSLN), who died in the guerrilla struggle against the Somoza dictatorship in the mid-1970s.

By their actions, these men preserved and reinforced in the Nicaraguan people a stubborn strain of irrepressibility and national pride. Finally, catalyzed into action early in 1978 by the brutal assassination of a prominent and beloved opposition newspaper editor, Nicaraguans of all classes rose up against the dictatorship of Anastasio Somoza Debayle and the system he represented. Eighteen months later, at a cost of approximately fifty thousand dead, the Nicaraguan revolution had triumphed. A brutal and selfish dictator had been overthrown, and a revolutionary government representing the aspirations of countless generations of Nicaraguans had finally come to power.

The Nicaraguan people were aware of the historic significance of their victory. In spite of the tremendous cost of the war, the mood in the country in July 1979 was one of near universal ecstasy. On July 20, the largest crowd ever assembled in Central America greeted the new government in the central plaza. As one young woman said a few days later, after detailing the loss of various family members, "That [the death and destruction] doesn't matter. The revolution triumphed! I feel as if I had just been born! Like a little baby with a whole life ahead of me!"

In a sense the people of Nicaragua *had* just been born. Almost immediately the new government took steps to reverse the centuries-old patterns of elite control and dominance. A substantial segment of the economy was nationalized, exports were put under strict government control, a massive literacy campaign was launched, and new ideas in health, housing, and public education were generated and put into practice. Though Nicaragua would continue to be dependent on exports, the old cycle of *dependency*, with all its human costs, would, it was hoped, be broken.

This book deals with the history of the Nicaraguan people and their social, economic, and political reality, past and present. It also examines the programs and policies – domestic and foreign – of the new revolutionary government. The themes of elite exploitation, foreign manipulation, national resistance, and revolutionary redirection receive special attention. I hope this approach will help the reader not only to appreciate why the Nicaraguan revolution took place but also to understand the motivations behind the various programs that the new government has begun to carry out.

NOTES

1. *1979 World Population Data Sheet* (Washington, D.C.: The Population Reference Bureau, 1979).

2. For a good discussion of *dependency*, see Ronald H. Chilcote and Joel C. Edelstein, "Alternative Perspectives of Development and Underdevelopment in Latin America," in their edited work, *Latin America: The Struggle with Dependency and Beyond* (New York: John Wiley and Sons, 1974), pp. 1–87.

2

Early History:
The Pre-Columbian Period
to the Mid-1930s

The history of Nicaragua is among the most turbulent and interesting in all of the Americas. If, on the one hand, it features incredible elite exploitation, mass suffering, and foreign interference, it also includes a significant element of popular resistance, national pride, and human nobility.

THE PRE-COLUMBIAN PERIOD

Even before the arrival of the Spaniards in the sixteenth century, the territory that we now call Nicaragua apparently was not a land of human tranquility. A demographic outpost of various Meso- and South American Indian groups, Nicaragua was an ethnically complex region. The most obvious dissimilarities were between the various indigenous tribes of South American origin that lived in the rain forests and savannahs to the east of the Central Cordillera and the Meso-American groups that inhabited the more hospitable western regions. The former, though primarily hunters and gatherers, also engaged in slash-and-burn agriculture, as do some of their descendants today. The more culturally sophisticated inhabitants of the western regions, on the other hand, were sedentary agriculturalists who raised corn, beans, and vegetables and lived in established towns with populations sometimes numbering in the tens of thousands. The western tribes spoke a variety of Meso-American languages reflecting several distinct waves of settlement from what is today Mexico and northern Central America. Though the western Indians rarely had anything to do with their more primitive counterparts across the mountains, contact and conflict among the tribes of the west were common. Warfare,

9

slavery, and involuntary tribute by the weak to the strong were among the basic ingredients of pre-Columbian life in the west. In a sense, then, many of the traits that characterized colonial rule existed long before the first *conquistadores* set foot in the land.

THE COLONIAL PERIOD: 1522-1822

The Spanish conquest of Nicaragua was an extension of the colonization of Panama, which began in 1508. Plagued by internal conflict, disease, and Panama's inhospitable natural environment, the Spaniards were not in a position to expand their control to the immediate north for well over a decade. It was only in 1522 that Gil González, commanding a small band of explorers under contract to the Spanish crown, finally set foot in Nicaragua. The purpose of his expedition—like that of other *conquistadores*—was to convert souls and to obtain gold and other riches from the native population. Considering that he managed to convert close to thirty thousand Indians, carry off nearly ninety thousand pesos worth of gold, and discover what appeared to be a water link between the Caribbean and the Pacific, González's venture into Nicaragua was a clear success.

It was not without its anxious moments, however. Though at first submissive, some Indians eventually decided to resist the bearded strangers. One of these was the legendary chief, Diriangén, from the region around what is today Granada. Several days after an initial meeting with González, in which he promised to bring his people to the Spaniard for conversion, Diriangén returned to attack the outsiders with several thousand warriors, causing them to retreat overland to the Pacific ocean.[1] To make matters worse, before they reached the safety of their Pacific fleet, González and his men were also set upon by warriors under the command of another chief, Nicarao. It was 1524 before the Spanish, under Francisco Hernández de Córdoba, returned to Nicaragua and imposed their control over the region.

The early years of the colonial period had a profound and lasting impact on the nature of Nicaraguan society and politics. The most important and tragic result of the conquest was demographic—the near total destruction of the large Indian population of the region. Incredible as it seems, it appears that Spanish chroniclers and early historians may have been fairly accurate when they reported that an original native population of around a million was reduced to tens of thousands within a few decades of the arrival of Gil González.[2] This incredible depopulation was the result of several factors. The outright killing of natives in battle, probably accounting for the demise of a few tens of thousands, was the least significant factor. Death by exposure to diseases brought to the New World by the Spaniards was much more important. The fact that Indians had little natural immunity to such common ailments as measles and influenza resulted in an immediate and dramatic reduction in their numbers throughout the Americas. It is likely that hundreds of thousands of Nicaraguan Indians perished of disease within a few decades.

Slavery was a third important factor that reduced Nicaragua's native population. Claims by writers of those times that four to five hundred thousand natives were gathered and exported into bondage during the first two decades of the colonial period seem to stand up to close scholarly investigation. The archives of the times show that there were enough slave ships of sufficient capacity making frequent enough trips to have accomplished this exportation.[3] The demand for slaves throughout the Spanish colonies—and especially in Peru in the 1530's—was very high. Though the Spanish themselves captured some slaves, many more were turned over to them by "friendly" Indian chiefs as a form of obligatory tribute. The life expectancy of these unfortunate souls was short. Many—sometimes 50 percent or more—died during the sea journey from Nicaragua to their intended destination. Most of the rest perished in slavery within a few years. As a result, supply never caught up with demand and, although the Spanish crown tried unsuccessfully to stop this lucrative trafficking in human life, the slave boom came to an end only when the resource was all but depleted. By the 1540s the Indian population of western Nicaragua appears to have plummeted to between thirty and forty thousand—and it declined gradually for several decades thereafter.

The result of this demographic holocaust is that Nicaragua today, instead of being a predominantly Indian country, is essentially mestizo in racial type and almost exclusively Spanish in language and other aspects of culture. Though most of the cities and towns of the country bear Indian names reflecting the culture of their founders, few of the people who walk their streets today are aware of what the names mean or who the original inhabitants were.

Another legacy of the colonial period—this one primarily political—was the rivalry between the principal cities of León, to the northeast of Lake Managua, and Granada, on the northern shore of Lake Nicaragua. Though both were founded by Francisco Hernández de Córdoba in 1524, they differed from each other in important cultural, social, and economic characteristics. As it was originally felt that Granada would be the political capital of the colony, the more "aristocratic" *conquistadores* chose to settle there. Spanish soldiers of lower rank and social status were packed off to León to defend the colony against incursions and claims by other Spanish adventurers from the north. As it turned out, however, León, not Granada, became the administrative center of the country, and Granada found itself forced to submit to the rule of a series of corrupt administrators based in what it considered a culturally inferior city. To make matters worse, there were significant differences in the economic interests of the two cities. The wealth of the self-styled aristocrats in Granada was based largely on cattle and on trade with the Caribbean via Lake Nicaragua and the San Juan River. Though cattle also were important in the region around León, many of the Leonese were also involved in such middle-class occupations as ship building, the procurement and sale of pine products, and government service. International trade in León was oriented almost entirely toward the Pacific. The Catholic church hierarchy, though stationed in the administrative center in León, sympathized with the aristocrats in Granada. Mutual jealousy and suspicion between the Leonese and Granadinos festered in a controlled form until independence allowed it to boil over into open warfare.

Curiously, the most flamboyant and prosperous years of the colonial period in Nicaragua were the first few decades – the time of the conquest and the slave trade. Once the Indian population had been depleted, the colony became an underpopulated backwater. Indeed, there was actually a severe manpower shortage, which forced some gold mines to close and caused landowners increasingly to switch from labor-intensive crop production to cattle raising. The economic foundation of this now underdeveloped colony was adequate to support the lifestyle of the landowning aristocrats in Granada and the merchants of León, but insufficient to provide for general prosperity.

To make matters worse, from the mid-seventeenth century on, the debilitated colony was frequently plagued by pirate attacks. As a result, trade via both the Caribbean and the Pacific was restricted and at times interrupted. By the mid-eighteenth century, the British, who were openly supportive of the pirates, became so bold as to occupy and fortify parts of the Caribbean coast. They maintained some claim over that region for well over a century.

INDEPENDENCE

The end of colonial rule in Central America simply added to the woes of the common Nicaraguan, for it meant the removal of the one external force that had kept the elites of León and Granada from sending their people into open warfare against each other. Mutual resentment between the two cities had flared up in 1811, a decade before the expulsion of the Spanish. When León, after first leading Granada into an insurrection against the crown, reversed its position and supported the royal authorities, it left the Granadinos in miserable isolation to receive the brunt of Spanish revenge. Nicaragua won its independence in stages: first as a part of the Mexican empire of Agustín de Iturbide in 1822, then as a member of the Central American Federation in 1823, and finally as an individual sovereign state in 1838. Throughout this period, the Leonese, who eventually came to call themselves Liberals, and the Granadinos, who championed the Conservative cause, squabbled and fought with each other over the control of their country. After 1838, the chaos and interregional warfare intensified. Presidents came and went as one group or the other imposed temporary control.

With Spain out of the way, other foreign powers began to interfere in Nicaraguan affairs, with the objective of dominating the interoceanic transit potential of the infant country. The British had long maintained a presence on the east coast. In the eighteenth century they had actually set up a form of protectorate over the Miskito Indians in that region. In the 1840s U.S. expansion to the Pacific coast of North America and the discovery of gold in California stimulated intense U.S. interest in Nicaragua as the site for an interoceanic transit route. Therefore, when the British moved to consolidate their control over the Miskito coast by seizing the mouth of the San Juan River, the United States became alarmed and protested vigorously to the British. In 1850 the two countries attempted to diffuse the potential for conflict by signing the Clayton-Bulwer Treaty, in which both sides forswore any unilateral attempt to colonize Central America or to dominate any transisthmian transit route.

THE WALKER AFFAIR

The treaty, however, failed to bring peace to Nicaragua. By the mid-1850s the two emerging themes of Nicaraguan political life – foreign interference and interregional warfare – converged to produce an important turning point and one of the most bizarre episodes in Central American history: the Walker affair. In spite of the Clayton-Bulwer Treaty, the clearly conflicting interests of the British and the Americans in the area had kept tension between the two countries at a high level. Both countries frequently took sides in Nicaraguan domestic politics – the British tending to support the Conservatives, and the Americans to support the Liberals. Finally, in 1854, the Liberals, who were at the time losing in a struggle to unseat the Conservatives, turned for help to a San Franciso-based soldier of fortune named William Walker.[4]

Though often depicted as a simple villain, Walker was an extremely interesting and complex individual. The son of a pioneer family from Tennessee, he was graduated from college and earned a medical degree while still in his teens. He then pursued a law degree, practiced that profession for a short while, turned to journalism, and finally became a soldier of fortune – all before he had reached his mid-thirties. In some senses he was an idealist. As a journalist he championed the cause of abolition and, like many people of that era, he was a firm believer in manifest destiny – the imperialist expansion of Yankee ideals, by force if necessary, beyond the boundaries of the United States.

In accordance with his pact with the Liberals, Walker sailed in June 1855 from California to Nicaragua with a small band of armed Californians. After some initial military setbacks he and his Liberal allies took Granada in October and set up a coalition government under a Conservative, Patricio Rivas. Almost from the start, the real power in the government was Walker himself, who rapidly began to implement a series of liberal developmentalist ideas that included the encouragement of foreign investment and the increased exploitation of Nicaraguan resources. In July 1856, Walker formally took over the presidency.

Initially Walker seems to have had at least the tacit support of the U.S. government. His entrance into the Nicaraguan civil war met with no serious resistance from Washington, which was quick to recognize the puppet government of Patricio Rivas. However, the British and the governments of the other Central American countries were appalled by this bald-faced Yankee attempt to create a U.S. outpost on the Central American isthmus. And many Nicaraguans of both parties became increasingly alarmed at the foreign takeover of their country. This was especially true in 1856 when Walker, the dictator-president, legalized slavery and declared English to be the official language. As a result, it was not long before the onset of a war in which Nicaraguans of both parties and, at one time or another, troops from all of the Central American republics (armed and backed financially by England, certain South American countries, and a variety of public and private interests in the United States) fought against the hated foreigners. In the spring of 1857, the U.S. government intervened to arrange a truce and to allow Walker to surrender and leave

Nicaragua. (Walker returned to Central America in yet another filibustering attempt in 1860, but he was captured by the British and turned over to the Hondurans, who quickly tried him and put him before a firing squad.) So important is the war against Walker in Nicaraguan patriotic lore that the independence day that *nicas* celebrate on September 14 is a commemoration of a decisive battle at San Jacinto against Walker and his U.S. troops.

THE CONSERVATIVE PERIOD: 1857–1893

For more than three decades following the defeat of Walker, the country enjoyed relative peace and stability. True, several thousand Indians lost their lives in 1881 in the tragic War of the Comuneros – a rebellion aimed at halting the takeover of their ancestral lands by wealthy coffee growers. But the elites of Nicaragua were temporarily at peace during this period. As a result of their association with the U.S. filibuster, the Liberals had been discredited. The Conservatives, therefore, were able to rule, without interruption and with only sporadic and halfhearted resistance from their traditional adversaries, from 1857 to 1893. A new constitution was adopted in 1857. Thereafter "elected" Conservative presidents succeeded each other at regular four-year intervals, breaking the old tradition of *continuismo* (an individual's self-perpetuation in power). The country was also blessed in this period with a relative lull in foreign interference, which came as a result of the completion in 1855 of a transisthmian railroad in Panama that temporarily took the pressure off Nicaragua as a focal point of interoceanic transit. And finally, during these decades Managua, which had become the capital in 1852, grew and prospered as a result of a coffee boom in that area.

ZELAYA AND ZELEDÓN

Conservative rule, however, was not to last. In 1893 the Liberals, under the leadership of José Santos Zelaya, joined dissident Conservatives in ousting the Conservative government of Roberto Sacasa. Three months later they overthrew the dissident Conservative whom they had initially placed in power and replaced him with Zelaya himself. For the next sixteen years Zelaya was not only the dictator of Nicaragua but also one of the most important figures in Central American regional politics.

Zelaya was a controversial and unjustly maligned figure. He is commonly described in U.S. textbooks on Central and Latin American history as a corrupt, brutal, cruel, greedy, egocentric, warmongering tyrant. In 1909 President William Howard Taft denounced him as "a blot on the history of Nicaragua." Careful examination of the facts, however, reveals that this depiction has much less to do with the reality of Zelaya's rule than with official U.S. frustration and resentment over the Liberal dictator's stubborn defense of national and Central American interests in the face of burgeoning U.S. interference in the affairs of the region following the Spanish-American War.[5]

Zelaya would be described more accurately as a relatively benevolent, modernizing, authoritarian nationalist. Born in Managua in 1853, the son of a Liberal coffee planter, he was educated at the Instituto de Oriente in Granada. At sixteen he was sent to France for further studies, and there he became imbued with the positivist philosophies of Auguste Comte and Herbert Spencer. When he returned to his homeland at nineteen, he immediately entered politics. Subsequently, as the young mayor of Managua, he set up a lending library and stocked it with the works of the French philosophers.

There is no doubt that, as dictator of Nicaragua, Zelaya used whatever means necessary to keep himself in power. Democracy did not exist; freedom of the press was often curtailed. It is also true that Zelaya was certainly no great social reformer. But there is little evidence of his alleged cruelty. His constitution of 1893 abolished the death penalty and he apparently made a practice of granting amnesty, after a decent interval, to captured opposition insurgents.

What is more important, Zelaya initiated many reforms in Nicaragua. In the first place, he worked to secularize Nicaraguan society; his constitution separated church and state and guaranteed freedom of religion and free secular education, and he financed the opening of new schools and the training of Nicaraguans abroad. By the end of his rule, the government was devoting approximately 10 percent of the budget to education.

Like other Latin Amercan positivist leaders of the time, he made a significant effort to modernize the economy. His government surveyed and opened new lands for the expansion of the coffee industry. It also fostered the collection and storage of information by setting up the National Archives and Museum, reorganizing the General Statistics Office, and conducting a national census. In addition, his government invested in the physical infrastructure of communication by purchasing steamships and building roads and telegraph lines. As a result of these modernizing efforts, there was, during the Zelaya period, a rapid increase in the production of such export commodities as coffee, bananas, timber, and gold.

In foreign affairs, Zelaya worked to defend Nicaraguan interests and to promote Central American reunification. More effective in the former than in the latter, he is best known for his success in getting the British to withdraw once and for all from the Miskito Coast. Although they had essentially agreed to withdraw in the 1860 Treaty of Managua, they had not done so. In 1894, Zelaya sent troops to the city of Bluefields, accepted the Miskito king's petition for incorporation, and expelled the protesting British consul from the territory. The British responded with a blockade of Nicaragua's Pacific port, but the United States – anxious to enforce the Monroe Doctrine – pressured them to back down and to accept full Nicaraguan sovereignty over the disputed area.

Zelaya's efforts at promoting Central American reunification, though unsuccessful, were significant. Capitalizing on a region-wide resurgence of Central American nationalism, stimulated in part by his own success in confronting the British on the Miskito Coast, Zelaya convened the Conference of Amapala in 1895, in which Nicaragua, Honduras, and El Salvador agreed to form a confederation called the *República Mayor* (the Greater Republic). A diplomatic representative was dispatched to the United States and received by President Grover Cleveland, and a constitution for this larger political entity was written in 1898. Unfortunately, before it could go into effect the incumbent government of El Salvador was overthrown and the new government withdrew from the union. The confederation subsequently collapsed.

Much is made in some accounts of the apparent fact that Zelaya was a disrupter of the peace in Central America. He did, indeed, invade neighboring Honduras on two occasions. However, it is equally true that he preferred to let the *República Mayor* collapse rather than send troops to El Salvador to hold it together by force. In addition, he settled boundary disputes with both of Nicaragua's neighbors through arbitration rather than by force. In the case of the boundary dispute with Honduras, he peacefully accepted a settlement that went against Nicaragua's claims.

Zelaya's downfall in 1909 was largely the result of a mounting conflict with the United States. It is important to remember that in that country at the turn of the century "imperialism" was not a dirty word. The Spanish-American War had given the United States a colonial empire and many Americans felt that their country had a legitimate colonial role to play in Central America. Zelaya's assertion as a regional leader and champion of Central American unity was, at least in part, a response to this threat – a response Washington resented. Zelaya also had the audacity to refuse to grant the United States canal-building rights that would have included U.S. sovereignty over certain Nicaraguan territory. As a result, the United States became involved in engineering Panamanian "independence" from Colombia and in 1903 signed the treaty it wanted with the new government it had helped create. A few years later the Americans became alarmed with rumors that Zelaya was negotiating with the British and the Japanese to build a second – and potentially competitive – canal through Nicaragua.

The upshot of these and other sources of friction between the United States and Zelaya was that Washington eventually let it be known that it would look kindly on a Conservative overthrow of Zelaya. In 1909, when the revolt finally took place in Bluefields, Zelaya's forces made the tactical mistake of executing two confessed U.S. mercenaries. The United States used this incident as an excuse to sever diplomatic relations and to send troops to Bluefields to ensure against the defeat of the Conservatives. Though he held on for a few more months, Zelaya was ultimately forced to accept the inevitable, to resign, and to spend the rest of his life in exile.

Before his resignation, Zelaya attempted to save the situation for his party by appointing a highly respected Liberal from León, Dr. José Madriz, to succeed him. The U.S. government, however, was determined that the Zelayista Liberals relinquish control. Washington refused to recognize the new government and early in 1910, when Madriz's troops succeeded in routing the rebel forces in an attempted thrust to the west and drove them back to Bluefields, the commander of U.S. forces in that town forbade government troops from attacking rebel positions. In the face of such foreign interference, it was impossible for the Liberals to win, much less to govern. On August 20, 1910, the Madriz government collapsed and was replaced by a puppet, pro-U.S. regime supported by the Conservatives and some opportunistic Liberal *caudillos* (leaders).

For the next two years (1910–1912), the economic and political situation deteriorated rapidly. The rebellion had disrupted the planting of crops and disturbed other sectors of the economy and, although the Madriz government had left the national treasury with a favorable balance, the new government squandered this resource almost immediately and began wildly printing paper money. Washington arranged private bank loans to its new client regime, but much of the loan money went almost immediately into the pockets of corrupt politicians. It was necessary to renegotiate loans and to allow the United States to become involved in the supervision of customs collection and the management of payment of the foreign debt.

The abysmal situation into which the country had fallen offended the national pride of many Nicaraguans, among them a young Zelayista Liberal, Benjamín Zeledón. A teacher, newspaperman, and lawyer, Zeledón had served Zelaya's government as a district judge in the newly liberated Atlantic territories, as an officer in the war with Honduras in 1907, as Nicaragua's representative to the Central American Court of Justice, and finally, at the age of thirty, as minister of defense. Under the Madriz government, he had continued as minister of defense and been elevated to the rank of general of the armies. In July 1912, when a group of dissident Conservatives rebelled against puppet president Adolfo Diaz, Zeledón and a group of Liberals joined in the uprising to rid Nicaragua of "the traitors to the Fatherland."

At first it appeared that the insurgents might win. Zeledón and his Liberal followers seized León and several other cities and cut communications to Managua. However, in the words of one U.S. observer of the times, "The U.S. could hardly permit the overthrow of the Conservative authorities. [If the rebels won] all of the efforts of the State Department to place Nicaragua on her feet politically and financially would have been useless, and the interests of the New York bankers . . . would be seriously imperiled."[6] Therefore, under the old pretext of protecting U.S. lives and property, U.S. Marines were sent into Nicaragua. Though resistance by dissident Conservatives was quickly overcome, Zeledón not only rejected U.S. demands that he, too, surrender but also warned the U.S. commander that he, his superiors, and the "powerful nation" to which he belonged would bear the "tremendous responsibility and eternal infamy that History will attribute to you for having employed your arms against the weak who have been struggling for the reconquest of the sacred rights of [their] Fatherland."[7]

Badly outnumbered by the combined U.S. and Nicaraguan government forces, Zeledón's troops were besieged and defeated, and he was captured by Nicaraguan troops. Though the United States was in a position to save Zeledón's life, Major Smedley D. Butler, in a telegram to his superiors, suggested that "through some inaction on our part someone might hang him."[8] Butler's advice was apparently taken, for, on the following day, the Conservative government announced that Zeledón had died in battle. Before the young patriot's body was buried, it was dragged through the little hamlet of Niquinohomo. There, by historical coincidence, a short, skinny, seventeen-year-old boy was among those who witnessed government troops kicking the lifeless form. This seemingly insignificant teenager—who later commented that the scene had made his "blood boil with rage"—was Augusto César Sandino.

THE U.S. OCCUPATION, THE NATIONAL GUARD, AND SANDINO

For most of the following two decades, Nicaragua was subjected to direct foreign military intervention. U.S. troops were stationed there from 1912 to 1925 and again from 1926 to 1933, an intervention apparently motivated by a variety of concerns. Relatively unimportant, though not negligible, was the desire to protect U.S. investment. The involvement of U.S. bankers in Nicaragua has been mentioned. There was also a sincere, if naive, belief in some circles that U.S. involvement could somehow help bring democracy to the country. The most important motivations, however, seem to have been geopolitical. U.S. decision makers felt it imperative to maintain a stable pro-U.S. government in Nicaragua, a country that, in addition to being an ideal site for a second transisthmian waterway, was located in the center of the U.S. sphere of influence in Central America.

During the first occupation, from 1912 to 1925, the United States ran Nicaraguan affairs through a series of Conservative presidents—Adolfo Diaz, Emiliano Chamorro, and Diego Manuel Chamorro. The relationship was symbiotic. The United States needed the Conservatives, and the Conservatives—who had neither the military strength nor the popular backing to maintain themselves in power—needed the United States. The Liberals were well aware that any attempt to regain power by means of an uprising would simply mean another unequal contest with the forces Zeledón faced in 1912, so an uneasy quiet prevailed.

The most notable product of the period was the Brian-Chamorro Treaty, signed in 1914 and ratified in 1916. By the terms of this document the United States acquired exclusive rights, in perpetuity, to build a canal in Nicaragua, a renewable ninety-nine-year lease to the Great and Little Corn Islands in the Caribbean, and a renewable ninety-nine-year option to establish a naval base in the Gulf of Fonseca. In return, Nicaragua was to receive payment of three million dollars. In reality, however, the U.S. officials who ran Nicaraguan financial affairs channeled much of that paltry sum into payments to foreign creditors. The aspects of the treaty dealing with the Corn Islands and the Gulf of Fonseca were hotly contested by El Salvador and Costa Rica, and the Central American Court of Justice decided in their favor. Though the United States had originally played a principal role in the creation of the court, it now chose to ignore its decision and, in so doing, contributed significantly to its collapse a few years later.

By the mid-1920s, U.S. decision makers had convinced themselves that the Conservatives were ready to carry on without the presence of U.S. troops. They were wrong. Within a few months of the first U.S. withdrawal in August 1925, conflicts flared up among the ruling Conservatives and, in 1926, the Liberals seized the initiative and staged a rebellion. The inevitable outcome was that the Conservatives were forced to turn again to Washington for salvation and U.S. troops returned to Nicaragua.

During the second occupation Washington showed greater skill and imagination in manipulating Nicaraguan affairs. It arranged a truce between the Liberals and the Conservatives that, among other things, provided for a free U.S.-supervised election in 1928. Though José María Moncada, the candidate of the majority Liberal party, won that contest, the United States was prepared to live with a Liberal president for, in the words of one scholar, the North Americans "controlled his regime from a number of points: the American Embassy; the Marines . . . ; the Guardia Nacional, with its United States Army Officers; the High Commissioner of Customs; the Director of the Railway; and the National Bank."[9] Under the circumstances, it no longer mattered whether the chief executive was a Liberal or a Conservative. Increasingly secure in this fact, the Americans in 1932 oversaw yet another free election won by yet another Liberal—this time, Juan B. Sacasa, ironically the same person who had led the Liberal uprising of 1926 that brought about the second occupation.

The importance of this period (1927–1933) lies much less in the individuals who happened to occupy the presidency than in the fact that, during these six years, forces were being shaped that were to have a powerful and paradoxical impact on Nicaragua for at least the next half century. This was the time of the germination of the Somoza dictatorship, which was to rule Nicaragua for over four decades, and of the reinvigoration of a revolutionary nationalist tradition that would ultimately overthrow that dictatorship in favor of a radically new system.

The revolutionary tradition was dramatically resuscitated by Augusto César Sandino, who led a long guerrilla war against U.S. and government forces during the second occupation of his country. Sandino was a fascinating person. Born in 1895 of a common-law union between a moderately well-to-do landowner and an Indian woman, he was accepted by his father and nurtured philosophically in the high principles that were supposed to form the basis of Liberal practice. He worked for his father until he was twenty-five, when he fled Nicaragua after a fight in which he wounded a man who had insulted his mother. He eventually ended up in Tampico, Mexico, working for Standard Oil of Indiana. There he absorbed some of the ideals of the Mexican Revolution – in particular the emphasis on the dignity of the Indian. In 1926 he returned to Nicaragua and found employment in a U.S.-owned gold mine. When the Liberal insurrection broke out that year, he organized a fighting unit and joined the insurgents. In 1927, after the rest of the Liberals had agreed to the U.S.-sponsored peace settlement, he chose to continue the battle against the puppet Conservative government. This decision inevitably brought him into conflict with U.S. troops and quickly turned his partisan crusade into a war of national liberation.

Though he wrote and spoke eloquently and profusely, Sandino was a man of action rather than a theorist. He did have certain ideas and opinions about the future of Nicaraguan politics and society. For instance, he advocated the formation of a popularly based political party and endorsed the idea of organizing land into peasant cooperatives. But more than anything else, he was a nationalist and an anti-imperialist. Quite simply, he found the U.S. occupation and domination of his country to be offensive and unacceptable. "The sovereignty and liberty of a people," he said, "are not to be discussed, but rather, defended with weapons in hand."[10]

In the struggle he led against U.S. and government troops, Sandino developed an effective set of guerrilla tactics through a process of trial and error. At first he used conventional military tactics, sending large groups of men into combat against an entrenched and well-equipped enemy. As a result, his troops initially took heavy casualties without inflicting serious damage. Learning from this mistake, he quickly developed the more classical guerrilla strategies of harassment and hit and run. In addition, he cultivated the support of the peasants in the regions in which he operated. They, in turn, served as an early warning communication network and as ad hoc soldiers during specific guerrilla actions.

The upshot of Sandino's activities was that the marines and government troops eventually found themselves bogged down in a costly Vietnam-type war that they simply could not win militarily. Practices such as the aerial bombardment of "hostile" towns and hamlets and the forced resettlement of peasant populations only intensified popular identification with the guerrilla cause. There were fluctuations in guerrilla activity and strength, but when the United States finally withdrew in January 1933, Sandino was still "as great a threat . . . as he had been at any previous point in his career."[11]

Ironically, the threat Sandino posed dissolved almost immediately after the Americans left. Because his major condition for peace had been the departure of the marines, Sandino signed a preliminary peace agreement, in February 1933, with the Sacasa government. Calling for a cessation of hostilities and a partial disarmament of the guerrillas, the document also guaranteed amnesty for Sandino's men and a degree of autonomy for those Sandinists who wished to settle in the territory along the Río Coco. In 1934 there were further peace negotiations. In the long run, however, Sandino was deceived, captured, and executed. But his daring stand against the foreign occupiers had been an example and had legitimized a set of tactics that were to be successfully employed by the Sandinist Front of National Liberation in overthrowing a U.S.-client dictatorship almost a half century later.

The other force that came into its own during the second U.S. occupation and had a profound impact on the future of the country was the National Guard of Nicaragua. Washington had long felt that what Nicaragua really needed was an apolitical constabulary that could maintain stability and create a healthy environment for political and economic development. Although a halfhearted attempt to create such a force had been made toward the end of the first occupation, the concept was not effectively implemented until the late 1920s. By then the United States was becoming increasingly tired of directly running Nicaragua's internal affairs. And, of course, there was the desire to "Nicaraguanize," if you will, the war against Sandino. Top priority, therefore, was placed on recruiting, training, arming, and equipping the *Guardia*. In the haste of the moment, safeguards aimed at maintaining the apolitical character of the guard were set aside. As the marines were leaving, command of this new "national" army passed from the Americans to a congenial, ambitious, English-speaking Nicaraguan politician, Anastasio Somoza García. Less than four years later, an elitist dictatorial system based on a symbiotic relationship between the now corrupted and thoroughly politicized National Guard and the Somoza family had come into being. This system was to plunder, degrade, and agonize the Nicaraguan people for more than four decades.

NOTES

1. A statue of Diriangén can be seen on the Carretera Sur in Managua.

2. For an excellent, scholarly examination of the early depopulation of Nicaragua, see David Richard Radell, "Native Depopulation and the Slave Trade: 1527–1578," in his *An Historical Geography of Western Nicaragua: The*

Spheres of Influence of León, Granada, and Managua, 1519–1965 (Ph.D. dissertation, University of California, Berkeley, 1969), pp. 66–80.

3. Ibid., pp. 70–80.

4. No known relation of the author of this volume.

5. For an excellent reexamination of Zelaya, see Charles L. Stansifer "José Santos Zelaya: A New Look at Nicaragua's Liberal Dictator," *Revista/Review Interamericana,* vol. 7, no. 3 (Fall 1977), pp. 468–485. The interpretation and much of the information in our short treatment of Zelaya is drawn from this fine source.

6. Dana G. Munro, *The Five Republics of Central America* (New York: Russell & Russell, 1967), p. 243.

7. A handwritten letter from Zeledón to Colonel J. H. Pendleton, Masaya, October 3, 1912. Xerox copy courtesy of Zeledón's grandson, Sergio Zeledón.

8. Major Smedley D. Butler as quoted in Richard Millett, *The Guardians of the Dynasty: A History of the U.S. Created Guardia Nacional de Nicaragua and the Somoza Family* (Maryknoll, New York: Orbis Books, 1977), p. 32.

9. Ralph Lee Woodward, Jr., *Central America: A Nation Divided* (New York: Oxford University Press, 1976), p. 200.

10. Though this is one of the best-known sayings from Sandino, we do not have the original citation.

11. Millett, *Guardians of the Dynasty,* p. 98.

3

Recent History:
The Somoza Era and
the Sandinist Revolution

In the Latin American context, Nicaraguan history since 1933 is unusual in at least two respects. First, though many other countries have suffered dictatorial rule, Nicaragua's forty-two-and-a-half-year subjugation to the Somozas was unique not only in its duration but also in its dynastic character. Nowhere else in Latin America has dictatorial power passed successively through the hands of three members of the same family. Second, Nicaragua is one of only a tiny handful of Latin American countries to have seriously attempted social revolution.

THE RISE OF ANASTASIO SOMOZA GARCÍA: 1933–1937

The founder of the Somoza dynasty, Anastasio Somoza García, was a complex and interesting individual. Born on February 1, 1898, the son of a moderately well-to-do coffee grower, "Tacho" Somoza was just short of thirty-five years when the departing marines turned over to him the command of the National Guard. His early ascent to this pivotal position of power was no mere accident. Intelligent, outgoing, persuasive, and ambitious, he was an unusual young man. He received his early education at the Instituto Nacional de Oriente and went on for a degree at the Pierce School of Business Administration in Philadelphia, where he perfected his English and met and married Salvadora Debayle, a member of one of Nicaragua's important aristocratic families. Upon his return to Nicaragua, he joined the Liberal revolt in 1926. Though he and his troops were ingloriously routed, he subsequently worked his way up in Liberal party politics, eventually serving as minister of war and minister of foreign relations.

A beguiling, gregarious young man with an excellent command of English, he got along well with the U.S. occupiers and was involved in the creation of the National Guard.

In the years immediately following the departure of the marines, Somoza worked efficiently to consolidate his control over the guard. In the wake of real or apparent anti-Somoza conspiracies, he purged various officers who might have stood in his way. Also, on February 21, 1934, he gave his subordinates permission to capture and murder Augusto César Sandino. In doing so, he not only eliminated a potential political rival but also endeared himself to many of the guardsmen, who harbored an intense hatred of the nationalist hero who had frustrated them for so long. Sandino's execution was followed by a mop-up operation in which hundreds of men, women, and children living in the semiautonomous region previously set aside for the former guerrillas were slaughtered. Finally, he encouraged guardsmen at all levels to engage in various forms of corruption and exploitative activities, thus isolating them from the people and making them increasingly dependent on their leader.

A sinister embrace: Anastasio Somoza García (left) and Augusto C. Sandino (right) a few days before Somoza's National Guard carried out the assassination of Sandino in 1934. (Photo courtesy of *Barricada*)

By 1936, Somoza was sufficiently sure of his control of the guard–and hence Nicaraguan politics–to overthrow the elected president, Juan B. Sacasa, and stage an "election" in which he was the inevitable winner. His inauguration on January 1, 1937, confirmed a fact that had long been apparent: In the wake of the U.S. occupation, the National Guard and its chief had become the real rulers of Nicaragua.

THE RULE OF ANASTASIO SOMOZA GARCÍA: 1937–1956

Somoza García was the dictator of Nicaragua for the next nineteen years. Occasionally, for the sake of appearance, he ruled through puppets, but for most of the period, he chose to occupy the presidency directly. In these years he developed an effective style of rule that was to characterize the Somoza dynasty until the late 1960s. The Somoza formula was really rather simply: maintain the support of the guard, cultivate the Americans, and co-opt important domestic power contenders.

The guard's loyalty was assured by keeping direct command in the family and by continuing the practice of psychologically isolating the guardsmen fom the people by encouraging them to be corrupt and exploitative. Accordingly, gambling, prostitution, smuggling, and other forms of vice were run directly by guardsmen. In addition, citizens soon learned that in order to engage in any of a variety of activities–legal or not–it was necessary to pay bribes or kickbacks to guard officers or soldiers. In effect, rather than being a professional national police and military force, the guard was a sort of Mafia in uniform, which served simultaneously as the personal bodyguard of the Somoza family.

Somoza also proved to be very adept in manipulating the Americans. Though Washington did occasionally react negatively to his designs to perpetuate himself indefinitely in power, the beguiling dictator was always able in the end to mollify U.S. decision makers. In addition to personal charm, he relied heavily on political obsequiousness in maintaining U.S. support. His regime consistently backed U.S. foreign policy. Washington's enemies were automatically Somoza's enemies, be they the Axis powers in the late 1930s and early 1940s or the Communists thereafter. The United States was allowed to establish military bases in Nicaragua during the Second World War and to use the country as a training area for the CIA-organized counterrevolution against Guatemalan president Jacobo Arbenz in 1954. Somoza even offered to send guardsmen to fight in Korea. In return, Somoza was lavishly entertained at the White House and received lend-lease funds to modernize the National Guard.

The dictator was also clever in his handling of domestic power groups. After the murder of Sandino and his followers, he adopted a more relaxed policy toward the opposition. Human rights and basic freedoms – for the privileged at least – were more generally respected. Whenever possible, the Conservative leadership was bought off – the most notable example being the famous "pact of the generals" in which the Conservative chiefs agreed to put up a candidate to lose in the rigged election of 1951 in return for personal benefits and minority participation in the government.

In addition, Somoza pursued developmentalist economic policies that emphasized growth in exports and the creation of economic infrastructure and public agencies such as the Central Bank, the Institute of National Development, and the National Housing Institute. Although the unequally distributed growth produced by this developmentalism did not do much for the common man, it did benefit Somoza significantly. In addition to providing opportunities to expand his originally meager fortune to around $50 million (U.S.) by 1956, it also created vehicles for employing and rewarding the faithful.

The rule of Anastasio Somoza García came to an abrupt and unexpected end in 1956 as the dictator was campaigning for "election" to a fourth term as president. On September 20 a young poet named Rigoberto López Pérez infiltrated a reception honoring the dictator and pumped five bullets point-blank into Somoza's corpulent hulk. In a letter he had sent to his mother, with instructions that it be opened only in the event of his death, López explained, "What I have done is a duty that any Nicaraguan who truly loves his country should have done a long time ago."[1]

If López, who was immediately shot by Somoza's bodyguards, thought his *ajusticiamiento* (bringing to justice) of the dictator would rid his country of Somozan rule, he was sadly mistaken. Although he died a few days later (in spite of the very best emergency medical assistance the Eisenhower administration could provide), Somoza already had taken steps to assure a smooth transition of rule within his immediate family. His sons, Anastasio and Luis, had been educated in the United States, the former at West Point and the latter at Louisiana State University, the University of California, and the University of Maryland. The more politically oriented Luis, president of the Congress at the time of his father's death, was constitutionally empowered to fill the presidency in the case of an unexpected vacancy. His more militarily inclined brother, Anastasio, had been head of the National Guard since 1955. When their father was killed, Luis automatically assumed the presidency, while his brother used the National Guard to seize and imprison all civilian politicians who might have taken steps to impede the dynastic succession. In 1957, Luis was formally "elected" to a term that would expire in 1963.

LUIS SOMOZA AND THE PUPPETS: 1957-1967

The decade 1957-1967 bore the mark of Luis Somoza Debayle, a man who seemed to enjoy "democratic" politics and appeared to be committed to the modernization and technical and economic development of his country. The older and wiser of the two Somoza sons, Luis was convinced that in order to preserve the system and protect the family's interests, the Somozas would have to lower their political and economic profile. His ideas and principles fitted neatly with the underlying philosophy and stated objectives of the U.S.-sponsored Alliance for Progress, which was being inaugurated with great fanfare in those years. Many of the programs Luis promoted in Nicaragua—public housing and education, social security, agrarian reform, etc.—coincided with the reform projects of the alliance.

In politics, Luis attempted to modernize the Liberal party, encouraging dissident Liberals to return to the fold and new civilian leaders to emerge. In 1959 he even had the constitution amended to prevent any member of his family—in particular his intemperate and ambitious younger brother, Anastasio—from running for president in 1963. From the end of his term until his death from a heart attack in 1967, Luis ruled through puppet presidents, René Schick Gutiérrez and Lorenzo Guerrero.

In spite of appearances, however, all was not well during this period. Alliance for Progress developmentalism, while creating jobs for an expanded bureaucracy and providing opportunities for the further enrichment of the privileged, had little positive impact on the lives of the impoverished majority of Nicaraguans, and "democracy" was a facade. Elections were rigged and the National Guard, as always, provided a firm guarantee that there could be no real reform in the political system.

Not surprisingly, therefore, there were a number of attempts to overthrow the system through armed revolt. Some of these attempts were made by younger members of the traditional parties, one was led by a surviving member of Sandino's army, and—from 1962 on—a number of operations were carried out by a new guerrilla organization, the Sandinist Front of National Liberation (FSLN). In response to these "subversive" activities, the dictatorship resorted to the frequent use of the state of siege and Washington helped increase the National Guard's counterinsurgency capabilities.

Though there is no doubt that Luis Somoza disapproved strongly of his younger brother's ambition to run for president in 1967, it is equally clear that there was little he could have done to have blocked it. Anastasio was, after all, the commander of the National Guard. Therefore, in June 1967 — after a blatantly rigged election — Anastasio Somoza Debayle became the third member of his family to rule Nicaragua. Luis's death a few months earlier and the bloody suppression of a mass protest rally shortly before the election symbolized the end of an era of cosmetic liberalization and the return to a cruder and harsher style of dictatorship.

ANASTASIO SOMOZA DEBAYLE'S FIRST TERM: 1967-1972

Anastasio differed from his older brother in several important respects. First, whereas Luis had attempted to build up a civilian power base in a rejuvenated Liberal party, Anastasio felt much more comfortable relying simply on military power. As chief of the *Guardia*, he relied on the old tradition of encouraging corruption and protecting officers from prosecution for crimes committed against civilians. In addition, whereas Luis and the puppets had surrounded themselves with a group of highly trained developmentalist technicians (*los minifaldas,* the miniskirts), Anastasio soon began replacing these skilled administrators with essentially unqualified cronies and political allies, many of whom were *Guardia* officers whom Somoza wanted to pay off or co-opt. Finally, whereas Luis had felt that, for the sake of image, the family should consolidate rather than expand its already vast fortune, his younger brother exercised no such restraint in using public office for personal enrichment. The result of all this was that by 1970 Somoza's legitimacy and civilian power base were evaporating rapidly and the government was becoming increasingly corrupt and inefficient.

According to the constitution, Anastasio was to step down from the presidency when his term expired in 1971. The dictator, however, was not bothered by such technicalities. Once in office he quickly amended the constitution to allow himself an additional year in office. Then, in 1971, with the advice and encouragement of U.S. Ambassador Turner Shelton, he arranged a pact with the leader of the Conservative party, Fernando Agüero, whereby he would step down temporarily and hand power over to a triumvirate composed of two Liberals and one Conservative (Agüero, of course) that would rule while a new constitution was written and an election for president was held. The transfer of power, which took place in 1972, was more apparent than real, as Somoza retained control of the guard. The inevitable result was that, in 1974, Somoza was "elected" to another term of office that was formally scheduled to last until 1981.

THE BEGINNING OF THE END: 1972-1977

The half-decade following the naming of the triumvirate in 1972 was a time of mounting troubles for the Somoza regime. Most of the responsibility for the growing systemic crisis lay in the excesses and poor judgment of the dictator himself. Somoza's first major demonstration of intemperance came in the wake of the Christmas earthquake of 1972, which cost the lives of more than ten thousand people and leveled a 600-square-block area in the heart of Managua. Somoza might have chosen to play the role of concerned statesman and patriotic leader by dipping into the family fortune (which, even then, probably exceeded $300 million [U.S.]) in order to help his distressed countrymen. Instead, he chose to turn the national disaster to short-term personal advantage. While allowing the National Guard to plunder and sell international relief materials and to participate in looting the devastated commercial sector, Somoza and his associates used their control of the government to channel international relief funds into their own pockets. Much of what they did was technically legal—the self-awarding of government contracts and the purchasing of land, industries, etc., that they knew would figure lucratively in the reconstruction—but little of it was ethically or morally uplifting.

It was at this point that open expressions of popular discontent with the Somoza regime began to surface. Although the triumvirate was technically in power when the quake struck, Somoza lost no time using the emergency as an excuse to push that body aside and proclaim himself head of the National Emergency Committee. There were many high-sounding statements about the challenge and patriotic task of reconstruction, but it soon became apparent that his corrupt and incompetent government was actually a major obstacle to recovery. The promised reconstruction of the heart of the city never took place. Popular demand for the building of a new marketplace to replace the one that had been destroyed went unheeded. Emergency housing funds channeled to Nicaragua by the Agency for International

Development (AID) went disproportionately into the construction of luxury housing for National Guard officers, while the homeless poor were asked to content themselves with hastily constructed wooden shacks. Reconstruction plans for the city's roads, drainage system, and public transportation were grossly mishandled. As a result, there was a series of strikes and demonstrations as the citizens became increasingly angry and politically mobilized.

It was at this point, too, that Somoza lost much of the support that he had formerly enjoyed from Nicaragua's economic elite. Many independent businessmen resented the way he had muscled his way into the construction and banking sectors. And most were angry at being asked to pay new emergency taxes at a time when Somoza–who normally exempted himself from taxes–was using his position to engorge himself on international relief funds. As a result, from 1973 on, more and more young people with impressive elite backgrounds joined the ranks of the Sandinist Front of National Liberation, and some sectors of the business community began giving the FSLN their financial support.

The second wave of excess followed a spectacularly successful guerrilla operation in December 1974. At that time, a unit of the FSLN held a group of elite Managua partygoers hostage until the government met a series of demands, including the payment of a large ransom, the publication and broadcast over national radio of a lengthy communiqué, and the transportation of fourteen imprisoned FSLN members and themselves to Cuba.[2] Enraged by this affront to his personal dignity, Somoza imposed martial law and sent his National Guard into the countryside to root out the "terrorists." In supposed pursuit of that objective, the guard engaged in extensive pillage, arbitrary imprisonment, torture, rape, and summary execution of hundreds of peasants.

Unfortunately for Somoza, many of the atrocities were committed in areas where Catholic missionaries happened to be stationed. As a result the priests and brothers could–and did–send detailed information about these rights violations to their superiors. The church hierarchy–already displeased with Somoza's decision in the early 1970s to extend his term of office beyond its original legal limit–first demanded an explanation from the dictator and then denouned the guard's rights violations before the world.

Somoza's flagrant disregard for human rights earned him considerable international notoriety. His excesses became the subject of hearings of the House of Representatives Subcommittee on International Relations[3] and a lengthy Amnesty International investigation.[4]

In all, by the middle of the decade, Somoza stood out as one of the worst human rights violators in the western hemisphere.

The year 1977 was a time of mounting crisis for the Somoza regime. That winter, the Episcopal Conference of Nicaragua devoted its New Year's message to a ringing denunciation of the regime's violations of human rights; the U.S.-based International Commission of Jurists expressed concern over the military trial of 111 individuals accused of working with the guerrillas; and Jimmy Carter, who had advocated in his campaign that the United States begin promoting human rights internationally, was inaugurated as president of the United States. Throughout 1977, the Carter administration pressed President Somoza to improve his human rights image. James Theberge, a right-wing, cold war warrior was replaced as U.S. ambassador to Nicaragua by the more humane and congenial Mauricio Solaún and military and humanitarian aid was used as a prod in dealing with the client regime. In response to the changing mood in Washington, Somoza, early that year, ordered the National Guard to stop terrorizing the peasantry. In September, he lifted the state of siege and reinstated freedom of the printed press.

Somoza's problems had been compounded in July, when the obese, hard-drinking dictator suffered a near fatal heart attack – his second – and had to be transported to the Miami Heart Institute, where he spent the next one-and-a-half months. This episode stimulated Nicaraguans of all political stripes to consider anew their country's political future. Even Somoza's aides, convinced that he would not return from Miami, began looting the treasury and plotting openly over the succession. As a result, when the dictator did recover, he was faced, upon his return to Nicaragua, with very serious problems within his own political household. Over the next three months he purged many of his former top advisors, including Cornelio Hüeck, president of the National Congress and national secretary of his own Liberal party.

By the last quarter of 1977, the Somoza regime was in deep trouble. Many Nicaraguans were frustrated and disappointed that nature had not been allowed to accomplish a second *ajusticiamiento* the previous summer. With the lifting of the state of siege and the reinstatement of freedom of the press, they could vent their feelings. Newspapers such as Pedro Joaquín Chamorro's *La Prensa* were free to cover opposition activities and discuss in vivid detail the past and present corruption and rights violations of the Somoza regime. In a single week that I spent in Nicaragua early in December, *La Prensa* ran articles on opposition meetings, a successful guerrilla action in the north, the fate of "missing" peasants in guerrilla areas, Somoza's relationship with a blood-plasm exporting firm (Plasmaféresis de Nicaragua), and the apparent embezzlement of AID funds by Nicaraguan Housing Bank officials. As a result, the regime's popular image dropped to an all-time low and Managua was alive with gossip and speculation about the impending fall of the dictator.

This situation undoubtedly emboldened the opposition. In October FSLN guerrillas attacked National Guard outposts in several cities and towns and a group of prominent citizens—professionals, businessmen, and clergy who subsequently became known as The Twelve—denounced the dictatorship and called for a national solution, which would include FSLN in any post-Somoza government. While several opposition groups spoke of a dialogue with Somoza, many, if not most, Nicaraguans felt, as did The Twelve, that

> there can be no dialogue with Somoza . . . because he is the principal obstacle to all rational understanding . . . through the long and dark history of *Somocismo,* dialogues with the dictatorship have only served to strengthen it . . . and in this crucial moment for Nicaragua, in which the dictatorship is isolated and weakened, the expediency of dialogue is the only political recourse that remains for *Somocismo.*[5]

Even that expediency was to evaporate shortly thereafter in the reaction to the assassination of Pedro Joaquín Chamorro.

THE WAR OF LIBERATION: 1978–1979

On January 10, 1978, as he was driving to work across the ruins of old Managua, newspaper editor Pedro Joaquín Chamorro died in a hail of buckshot fired at close range by a team of professional assassins. This dramatic assassination was the final catalyst for a war that culminated in the complete overthrow of the Somoza system eighteen months later. Though this struggle is often referred to as a civil war, many Nicaraguans are quick to point out that that term does not fit because it implies armed conflict between two major national factions. The Nicaraguan war, they maintain, was actually a "war of liberation" in which an externally created dictatorial system supported almost exclusively by a foreign-trained personal army was overthrown through the concerted effort of virtually all major groups and classes in the country. Somoza, they say, was simply "the last marine."

The assassination of Chamorro—a humane and internationally renowned journalist who, little over three months before, had received Columbia University's María Moors Cabot Prize for "distinguished journalistic contributions to the advancement of inter-American understanding" – enraged the Nicaraguan people. Though it is possible that Somoza may not have been directly responsible for the crime, few of his countrymen took that possibility seriously. Immediately after the assassination, angry crowds surged through the streets of Managua burning Somoza-owned buildings and shouting anti-Somoza slogans. Later, when it became apparent that the official investigation of the murder was to be a cover-up, the chambers of commerce and industry led the country in an unprecedented general strike that lasted for more than two weeks with 80 to 90 percent effectiveness. Strikes of this sort had almost always proven fatal to Latin American dictatorships; but not so in the case of Anastasio Somoza, for he had the firm support of a thoroughly corrupt military establishment that simply could not afford to risk a change of government. When it became clear that it was hurting the Nicaraguan people more than their well-protected dictator, the strike was called off.

The fact that the strike was over, however, did not mean that Somoza's troubles had ended. To the contrary, Nicaraguans of all classes had experienced the thrill and surge of pride that came with defying the dictator and were, therefore, in no mood to let things slip back to normal. For the next several months, acts against the regime came in various forms. There were daring and quite successful FSLN attacks on National Guard headquarters in several cities, mass demonstrations, labor and student strikes and – a new factor – civil uprisings in urban areas.

The events of February in Monimbó – an Indian neighborhood in Masaya – were a preview of what was to happen in most Nicaraguan cities that September, when poorly armed civilians rose up against the dictatorship only to be brutally pounded into submission. Fighting in Monimbó broke out between the local inhabitants and the guard on February 10, the one-month anniversary of the Chamorro assassination, and again on February 21, the forty-fourth anniversary of Sandino's assassination. On the second occasion, the inhabitants set up barricades, hoisted banners declaring Monimbó to be a free territory, and held the guard back for almost a week with a pathetic assortment of weapons consisting of homemade bombs, 22-caliber rifles, pistols, machetes, axes, rocks, and clubs. Before it could declare Monimbó "secure" on February 28, the regime had to use a force of 600 heavily armed men backed by two tanks, three armored cars, five 50-caliber machine guns, two helicopter gunships, and two light planes.[6] In the process, the neighborhood was devastated and many dozens, perhaps hundreds, of civilians were either killed outright or arrested and never seen again.

Meanwhile, Somoza was defiantly reiterating his intention to stay in power until the expiration of his term of office in 1981. Swearing that he would never resign before that time, he sputtered angrily at one point that "They will have to kill me first. . . . I shall never quit power like Fulgencio Batista in Cuba or Pérez Jiménez in Venezuela. I'll leave only like Rafael Leonidas Trujillo of the Dominican Republic. . . . That is, dead."[7] In a calmer mood on another occasion he commented, "I'm a hard nut. . . . They elected me for a term and they've got to stand me."[8]

The Nicaraguan people, however, were not about to stand Somoza for another two years, much less wait until 1981 to participate in yet another rigged election – the "solution" that the United States, at that time, was promoting. Acts of passive resistance and violent opposition continued. July was a particularly active month. On July 5, The Twelve returned from exile, in defiance of the dictator's wishes, and were greeted as heroes by huge crowds at the airport and throughout the country. On July 19, "over 90% of the businesses in Managua and 70% of those in the country as a whole" answered the Broad Opposition Front's (FAO) call for a one-day, show-of-strength general strike.[9] And, on July 21, Fernando Chamorro, an automobile sales executive, carried out a daring, one-man rocket attack on *El Bunker* – Somoza's fortified, subterranean office and living quarters – where Somoza was holding a cabinet meeting.

The situation finally came to a head in August. Early that month, the Nicaraguan people heard to their astonishment that Jimmy Carter had sent Somoza a private, but subsequently leaked, letter late in July congratulating him for his promises to improve the human rights situation in Nicaragua. Exasperated by this news and determined to recapture the initiative, the FSLN decided to set in motion plans for its most spectacular guerrilla action to date, the seizure of the National Legislative Palace in the heart of old Managua. According to Eden Pastora, the "Commander Zero" who led the operation, the FSLN had been outraged by Carter's letter. "How could he praise Somoza while our people were being massacred by the dictatorship? It was clear it meant support for Somoza, and we were determined to show Carter that Nicaraguans are ready to fight Somoza, the cancer of our country. We decided, therefore, to launch the people's struggle."[10]

Operation Pigpen, which began on August 22, was as successful as it was daring. Dressed as elite guard of Somoza's son, Anastasio III, twenty-five young FSLN guerrillas, most of whom had never set foot in the National Palace, drove up in front, announced that "the chief" was coming, brushed past regular security personnel, and took command of the whole building in a matter of minutes. Before most of them even realized what was happening, more than fifteen hundred legislators, bureaucrats, and others conducting business in the palace were hostages of the FSLN. It was another humiliating defeat for Somoza. After fewer than forty-eight hours of bargaining the FSLN commandos extracted a stinging list of concessions from the dictator, including $500,000 (U.S.) in ransom, airtime on radio and space in the press for an anti-Somoza communiqué, government capitulation to the demands of striking health workers, and guarantee of safe passage out of the country for fifty-nine political prisoners and the guerrillas. The governments of Panama and Venezuela vied with each other for the honor of providing the FSLN commandos with air transportation and asylum. And thousands of Nicaraguans cheered the new national heroes on the way to the airport as they departed.

The success of the FSLN palace operation triggered massive acts of defiance by Nicaraguan society as a whole. On August 25, the Broad Opposition Front (composed, at that time, of most of Nicaragua's political parties and organizations) demanded Somoza's resignation and declared another nationwide strike, which paralyzed the country for almost a month. Simultaneously, Monimbó-style civil uprisings occurred in cities throughout the country, including Masaya, Matagalpa, Managua, Chinandega, León, Jinotepe, Diriamba, and Estelí. Once again, young people armed only with an assortment of pistols, hunting rifles, shotguns, homemade bombs, and the moral support of their elders erected paving block barricades and battled elite units of Somoza's National Guard. Several towns—including León, the traditional stronghold of Somoza's Liberal party—held out for a week or more against terrible odds.

The outcome, however, was inevitable. Somoza and his hated National Guard knew that they were in a struggle for their very lives. The guard, therefore, fought with unusual ferocity and vengeance, leveling large sections of several cities and taking the lives of between three thousand and five thousand people. The dictator's own son and heir apparent, Harvard-educated Anastasio Somoza Portocarrero, led the ground operations. After first "softening up" insurgent cities and neighborhoods with aerial strafing and bombardment, government troops moved in to "mop up." As most of the active insurgents usually had withdrawn by the time the troops took the cities, the mop-up operations frequently involved the mass summary execution of noncombatants—in particular those males who had the misfortune of being of fighting age.[11]

The events of August and September 1978 caused Nicaraguans

on both sides to do some hard thinking. For his part, Somoza apparently began to realize that his dictatorial system might be doomed. In the next ten months, he and his associates worked feverishly to liquidate assets and transfer money abroad. At the same time, however, Somoza displayed an outward determination to hold on and to crush the "Communist . . . jerks." He announced plans to double the size of the guard and bragged openly that, in spite of a U.S. arms freeze, he was having little trouble getting the arms and ammunition he wanted on the open market (mainly from Israel and Argentina).

Somoza was also quite clever in manipulating the United States in his efforts during this period to buy time. The September uprisings had caused the Carter administration, at least temporarily, to feel that Somoza might not be able to survive until 1981. This feeling was accompanied by a growing sense of alarm that Nicaragua might turn into "another Cuba."[12] The dictator played very effectively upon these cold war fears. His lobbyists in Washington argued passionately that Somoza was a loyal ally of the United States, about to be overthrown by Cuban-backed Communists. And from October to January Somoza himself toyed with a U.S.-led mediation team from the Organization of American States (OAS) while it attempted to negotiate a transition agreement between Somoza and the small handful of traditional politicians who were still willing to make deals with the dictator. Dangling the idea of a national plebiscite before the OAS team and his traditional "opponents," Somoza did not kill the mediation process until January 1979, when he apparently was sufficiently confident of his own military strength that he no longer needed such charades.

Ironically, even though the Carter administration reacted with anger to Somoza's treachery by reducing its diplomatic presence in Managua and by finally withdrawing its small team of military attachés, the Americans, too, apparently felt that Somoza had weathered the storm. In May 1979, the administration once again aided the dictator by reversing an earlier position and allowing a $66 million International Monetary Fund (IMF) loan for Nicaragua to be approved without U.S. opposition.

Meanwhile, the Nicaraguan people had also learned some valuable lessons from the events of August and September 1978. It was clear that neither general strikes nor poorly armed mass uprisings would drive Somoza from office. The dictator and his guard had demonstrated their willingness to slaughter and destroy in order to preserve their position. The next uprising, therefore, would have to be led by a larger, well-trained, well-armed guerrilla force. Accordingly, for the next eight months, the Sandinist Front of National Liberation worked to prepare itself for a massive final offensive. The recruitment and training of young men and women – primarily students from urban areas – went on at a frenetic pace as the regular FSLN army expanded from several hundred to several thousand. Members of the opposition – particularly The Twelve – traveled throughout the world explaining the Sandinist cause and soliciting donations. Money received from various governments in Latin America, the Social Democratic parties of Western Europe, and solidarity groups in the United States and elsewhere was used to purchase modern, light, Western-made weapons on the international arms market. In March 1979, the FSLN, which formerly had been divided into three factions, finally coalesced under one nine-man directorate and issued a joint declaration of objectives. The stage was set for the final offensive.

After a false start in Estelí in April, the real final offensive was declared early in June 1979. Paving-block barricades were erected in poor neighborhoods throughout the country and National Guard outposts were overcome one by one as the dictator's control of the country shrank. In mid-June a broad-based government-in-exile was announced by the FSLN. Alarmed by the near certainty of a popular victory, the United States tried various schemes to block such an outcome, including a request to the OAS that a peacekeeping military

Fighting at the barricades. Ironically, the *adoquín* paving blocks used to construct the barricades had been made in the dictator's own factory. (Photo courtesy of *Barricada*)

force be sent to Managua. When this proposal for armed intervention was unanimously rejected, the Carter administration finally began to deal directly with the provisional government. Using various threats and promises, it tried unsuccessfully to force the FSLN to agree to preserve the National Guard—albeit in an altered form—and to include "moderates," such as members of the guard and Somoza's party, in the government. When the FSLN refused, Washington finally accepted the inevitable and arranged for the departure of Somoza to Miami on July 17. A day later, the provisional government took the oath of office in a ceremony held in León and, on July 19, the FSLN entered Managua and accepted the surrender of most of what was left of the National Guard. Ecstatic crowds tore the statues of Anastasio Senior and Luis Somoza from their pedestals and dragged the broken pieces triumphantly through the streets. On July 20, the provisional government entered the capital and appeared in the main plaza to receive the acclaim of a jubilant and grateful people. The Sandinist insurrection had won unconditionally.

The triumph—July 19, 1979.
(Photo courtesy of *Barricada*)

THE NEW REVOLUTIONARY ORDER

The government that the FSLN installed when it seized power reflected the pluralistic, multiclass nature of the insurrection. The Junta of National Reconstruction included two militants of the FSLN, Daniel Ortega Saavedra and Moises Hassan; an author-educator and member of the Group of Twelve, Sergio Ramírez Mercado; a prominent businessman, Alfonso Robelo Callejas; and the aristocratic Violeta Barrios de Chamorro, wife of the martyred editor of *La Prensa*.[13] The first cabinet contained a variety of people ranging from FSLN militants to Christian Democrats and former independent Liberals and Conservatives. The Catholic church, which had played an important role in the revolution, was represented by the guerrilla-poet, Father Ernesto Cardenal, and Maryknoll Father Miguel d'Escoto.

In spite of the rather heterogeneous nature of the junta and its cabinet, there was little visible intragovernmental factionalism. This was due to the fact that, in reality, the government was ruling Nicaragua at the pleasure of the country's only real power factor, the nine-man directorate of the FSLN. In the wake of the overthrow of Somoza, the FSLN indisputably dwarfed all other political groups in both popularity and organization. The red and black of the Sandinist movement were Nicaragua's new patriotic colors. While most of the old parties and interest organizations were weak, dying, or dead, Sandinist "popular organizations" had burgeoned. There were grass-roots Sandinist Defense Committees (CDSs) in practically every neighborhood and hamlet in the country. Other FSLN mass organizations included the Sandinist Youth, the Sandinist Workers' Central (CST), Luisa Amanda Espinosa Association of Nicaraguan Women (AMNLAE), and the Rural Workers' Association (ATC). The FSLN published a national daily newspaper, *Barricada*, and operated television and radio networks. Most important, military power was now an exclusive monopoly of the FSLN, with its Sandinist Popular Army, Sandinist Police, and Sandinist Popular Militia. Under these circumstances, it was unlikely that any Nicaraguan government in the foreseeable future would fail to place major emphasis on a rapid transformation of the country's social structures in behalf of the common citizen.

The reconstruction tasks confronting the new government were staggering. The human cost of the war was approximately fifty thousand dead, one hundred thousand wounded, forty thousand orphaned, one-fifth of the population homeless, and one-third of the work force jobless. In addition, the country's economic infrastructure had been wantonly devastated or looted by the departing dictator and his accomplices. Many of the nonmovable assets of the former ruling elite had been mortgaged (to the public and private banks they controlled) at as much as two to three times their value. Most of the money from short-term, high-interest loans contracted in the previous year by the Somoza government from private banks abroad had simply evaporated. Finally, in apparent retaliation for the three general strikes called by the chambers of commerce and industry, Somoza had used his air force to destroy many opposition-owned industrial and commercial establishments. Nicaragua was a war-torn country, close to bankruptcy with a $1.6 billion foreign debt on which large payments were due almost immediately.

Even before they came to power, the junta and the FSLN leadership had expressed their determination to create a "new Nicaragua" with a new type of social revolution appropriate to the internal and international realities of that small but proud country.[14] Above all, the government was determined to carry out a genuine social revolution with a rapid reordering of the relationship between classes and to do so, if possible, within the framework of Western pluralist democracy.

The record of the new government in reinstating and protecting civil and political liberties—though not unflawed—was remarkable under the circumstances. As they had promised before coming to power, the Sandinists were compassionate in victory. Though there were some isolated incidents of impromptu *ajusticiamientos,* capital punishment was immediately outlawed and most of the more than seven thousand suspected war criminals and Somoza accomplices who had been rounded up after the victory were carefully investigated and either released or brought to trial before special courts. The maximum penalty for those convicted was a thirty-year jail sentence. Freedom of the press was quickly reinstated and independent newspapers and radio stations were soon competing with FSLN organs for the attention of the public. Though one paper, *El Pueblo,* was closed for its alleged attempts to sabotage the revolution, the country's leading daily, *La Prensa,* reappeared and then split into two papers, *El Nuevo Diario* (which usually supported the government) and an essentially new *La Prensa* (which criticized the direction of the revolution and vocalized the fears of the privileged minority). Finally, the new regime generally respected the right to organize politically. Though the discredited Liberal and Conservative parties were essentially dead and the FSLN, with its associated neighborhood and interest organizations, was by far the country's most important political force, several elite-oriented microparties also functioned with relative freedom.

The economic programs of the new government were tailored more to Nicaraguan reality than to ideology. For the short run at least, the revolutionaries envisioned a mixed economy. Immediately after the victory the holdings of the Somozas and their accomplices were confiscated. In one stroke, the state had become the owner of over 20 percent[15] of the country's arable land and 154 commercial and industrial establishments. Soon after, following the example set by Costa Rica thirty years earlier, the government nationalized the banking and insurance industries. The immediate problem, then, was not how to nationalize more property but, rather, how to manage that which had already been seized. It was decided that honest and efficient private enterprises – industrial, commercial, and agricultural – would be allowed to function as long as they acted in the public interest.

In agriculture, there would be various types of land tenure and use. Large private enterprises could continue to operate as long as they did so efficiently. But the export products grown on them would now be sold directly to the new Institute of Internal-External Commerce, which would market them abroad. In this way the government could collect revenues that would be plowed back into social and economic projects. Meanwhile confiscated lands would be used for state farms and cooperatives.

In the social realm, the government moved quickly to redress the grievances of the neglected common people. Highly visible, labor-intensive public works projects served the dual purpose of giving the people the parks, recreation centers, public markets, sidewalks, and roads the Somoza elite had long denied them while, at the same time, providing employment for many thousands of the country's jobless, unskilled workers. Other social programs included the massive literacy campaign of 1980, universal vaccination drives, the training of paramedics to take health care to the poor, rent control, and agrarian reform. In many of these endeavors, the Sandinist Defense Committees proved to be invaluable as volunteer, grassroots facilitators.

In foreign policy, the revolutionary government was determined to follow a course of action appropriate to Nicaraguan reality. Given its geopolitical position as a tiny country in the back yard of the United States and its need for access to U.S. markets for its primary products, the new government was intent on retaining good relations with Washington. On the other hand, it was equally determined never again to allow Nicaragua to be a client state. What is more, the Nicaraguans naturally admired and were determined to have friendly

Unskilled workers constructing a huge children's park in the center of old Managua, November 1979. (Photo by the author)

relations with other social revolutionary governments such as those of Vietnam and Cuba. As a result, the revolutionary government chose to adopt a nonaligned posture aimed at the preservation of full national sovereignty and the avoidance of conflict with other nations.

NOTES

1. Rigoberto López Pérez as quoted in Mayo Antonio Sánchez, *Nicaragua Año Cero* (Mexico: Editorial Diana, 1979), p. 96.

2. For an FSLN account of this action and a transcript of the communiqué, see Comando Juan José Quezada, *Frente Sandinista: Diciembre Victorioso* (Mexico: Editorial Diogenes, S.A., 1976).

3. U.S., Congress, House, Committee on International Relations, Subcommittee on International Organizations, *Human Rights in Nicaragua, Guatemala and El Salvador: Implications for U.S. Policy,* hearings, June 8, 9, 1976 (Washington, D.C.: U.S. Government Printing Office, 1976).

4. Findings summarized in *Amnesty International Report, 1977* (London: Amnesty International Publications, 1977), pp. 150–153.

5. *Apuntes para el Estudio de la Realidad National*, no. 1 (Junio 1978), p. 9.

6. Ibid., p. 22.

7. "Somoza Rules out Early Departure," *Central America Report*, vol. 5, no. 12 (March 20, 1978), p. 95.

8. "The Twelve: Nicaragua's Unlikely Band of Somoza Foes," *Washington Post*, July 23, 1978.

9. "Nicaragua Strike," *Central America Report*, vol. 5, no. 29 (July 24, 1978), p. 231.

10. "Rocking Nicaragua: The Rebels' Own Story," *Washington Post*, September 3, 1978, p. C-1.

11. Organization of American States, Inter-American Commission on Human Rights, *Report on the Situation of Human Rights in Nicaragua* (Washington, D.C.: General Secretariat of the OAS, 1978).

12. For more detailed analysis of U.S. policymaking in this period, see William LeoGrande, "The Revolution in Nicaragua: Another Cuba?" *Foreign Affairs*, vol. 58, no. 1 (Fall 1979), pp. 28–50; and Richard R. Fagen, "Dateline Nicaragua: The End of an Affair," *Foreign Policy*, no. 36 (Fall 1979), pp. 178–191.

13. Though two junta resignations did occur early in 1980, those vacancies were quickly filled in such a way as to preserve the pluralistic nature of the body. See Chapter 6.

14. See, for instance, Sergio Ramírez, "What the Sandinistas Want," *Caribbean Review*, vol. 8, no. 3 (Summer 1979), pp. 24–27, 49–52.

15. Before the liberation, most estimates were that Somoza and his associates owned around 50 percent of the arable land. However, when a careful check was made by the new government it was discovered that those figures were inaccurately high.

4

The Economic Dimension

When the revolutionary government that replaced the Somoza regime in 1979 drew up its first comprehensive economic plan – *The 1980 Program for Economic Reactivation in Benefit of the People* – it was well aware that it faced a stark reality. "We are confronting," the government observed, "the effects of a hundred years of dependent capitalism which expresses itself in the appropriation of the national wealth by an extremely small group, leaving the vast majority of the population in misery and ignorance."[1] The term *dependent capitalism* as used in this statement is not a rhetorical or demogogic expression. It refers to an objective reality – a socioeconomic pattern predominant throughout Latin America that seems to persist whether the political form of the moment be liberal "democracy" (for example, Colombia from the late 1950s on), one-man dictatorship (the Dominican Republic under Rafael Trujillo or Venezuela under Marcos Pérez Jiménez), progressive military rule (Peru, 1968–1975), or rightist military dictatorship (Brazil after 1964 or Chile after 1973).

There is a profound difference between what is loosely called free enterprise or capitalism in the United States and its counterpart in Latin America. Capitalism in the United States coexists with relatively high levels of social justice precisely because it is dependent on the bulk of the American people as consumers. Most of what U.S. industry produces is consumed in the United States. The economic system, therefore, would collapse if the majority of citizens were exploited to the extent that they could no longer consume at relatively high levels. Quite the opposite is true in Latin America, where the so-called "capitalist" economies are overwhelmingly externally oriented, placing great emphasis on the production of products for export. Under these dependent capitalist systems the common citizen is important as a cheap and easily exploitable source of labor rather than as a consumer. Therefore, there is little or no economic incentive for the

47

privileged classes that dominate most Latin American governments to make the sacrifices necessary to improve the conditions of the majority of the people.

While prerevolutionary Nicaragua was not at all unusual as an example of a society distorted by dependent capitalism, it was nevertheless an exceptionally and strikingly tragic case. Unlike certain other countries – such as Bolivia, where natural resources are in relatively short supply – Nicaragua is, and always has been, a land of impressive economic potential. The population/land ratio is very favorable. Not only is Nicaragua the largest of the five Central American countries, it is the least densely populated, with fewer than 20 persons per square kilometer as opposed to 45 for the region as a whole and approximately 210 for El Salvador. The land itself is rich and varied, with different soil, climatological, and altitude characteristics suitable for the production of a wide variety of crops and livestock. The country's many rivers and volcanos offer easily exploitable sources of both hydroelectric and geothermal energy, and internal waterways facilitate inexpensive domestic transportation and present the possibility of exploitation as part of some future transoceanic waterway. Nicaragua has both Caribbean and Pacific coastlines, providing direct access not only to the food and mineral resources of the seas but also to the major markets of the world. The country has significant timber resources – from pine forests in the highlands to hardwood stands in the lowland tropics. Among the known mineral assets are silver and, particularly, gold. Finally, the Nicaraguan people, with their relatively homogeneous culture and language and their indomitable spirit and *joie de vivre*, are themselves a very important national asset.

The tragedy – indeed the gross injustice – of prerevolutionary Nicaragua was that in spite of all this potential and some apparent signs of "development", such as frequent spurts in gross national product (GNP), the vast majority of the Nicaraguan people, even in the late 1970s, led a stark existence while a small, privileged minority monopolized and misused the national resources to their own nearly exclusive benefit. This fact is illustrated by income distribution figures for the late 1970s that show that 20 percent of the population (i.e., the upper and middle class) received 60 percent of the national income while 80 percent (the lower classes) were expected to make do with the other 40 percent. The poorest 50 percent had access to only 15 percent of the national income, for an average of a little more than a couple of hundred dollars per person per year.[2]

EVOLUTION OF THE ECONOMIC SYSTEM

The best way to understand the inequities of the Nicaraguan economic system is to examine its historical roots. Nicaraguan economic history prior to the Sandinist Revolution is divisible into four distinct time spans: (1) the colonial period, from the 1520s to the 1820s; (2) the first half century of independence, from the 1820s through the 1870s; (3) the period of primitive dependent capitalism, from the late 1870s through the 1940s; and (4) the rise of modern dependent capitalism, from the 1950s through the 1970s.

The Colonial Economy

When the Spaniards arrived in western Nicaragua in the early sixteenth century they found a relatively advanced agrarian society. The approximately one million native inhabitants of the region—descendants of colonizers and refugees from the Mayan and Aztec civilizations to the north—lived in villages and cities ranging in population from a few hundred to tens of thousands. This was a feudal society, with chiefs, subchiefs, and commoners, in which tribute flowed from the lowly to the lofty. However, land was held collectively and each inhabitant of the villages and cities had access to a designated plot nearby. The rich soils of the region yielded agricultural products in abundance ranging from corn, cassava, and chili to beans, tobacco, and a variety of vegetables. Each population center had one or more local markets at which agricultural products were sold. Though periodic crop failure and intertribal warfare undoubtedly inflicted occasional acute hardship, the economy in general was relatively self-sufficient and self-contained. The market system, intraregional trade, and general access to rich agricultural lands provided the material wherewithal for the satisfaction of basic human needs.

The Spanish conquest, as I noted earlier, had an immediate and devastating impact on this economic system. Superimposing themselves on the existing feudal structure, the *conquistadores* demanded tribute in gold and, when that was depleted, Indian slaves. Within a few decades the near total destruction of the native population through death by contact with European diseases and the export of slaves created a severe manpower shortage that all but destroyed the labor-intensive agricultural base of the region's economy. To be sure, some lands remained under intensive cultivation throughout the colonial period, providing some export products such as corn and cacao and food to meet the region's much reduced internal demand. But, for the most part, the rich lands of Nicaragua reverted to jungle or were exploited for the raising of cattle to produce hides, tallow, and salted meat for sale to other colonies.

In a few decades, therefore, the economy had become essentially externally oriented. In addition to the sale of corn, cacao, and cattle products, the tiny Spanish elite accrued wealth through the exploitation of forest products, shipbuilding, and intermittent gold mining—all to meet external rather than internal demands. The underpopulation of the colony and the concentration of wealth in the hands of the privileged classes of León and Granada made Nicaragua a prime target for attacks by pirates from England and elsewhere in Europe, further contributing to the region's status as a colonial backwater. The process of underdevelopment had begun.

The First Half Century of Independence

The partial interruption of foreign dominance resulting from the disintegration and eventual collapse of Spanish colonial rule in the early nineteenth century was reflected in important changes in the Nicaraguan economic system. It is true that British traders were quick to provide the landed elite with an outlet for their traditional export products, but the relative political anarchy and international isolation of the first half century of independence also encouraged the growth of a number of other types of economic activity. There was a rapid growth in the number of self-sufficient peasant farms or *huertas*. A fragile, indigenous marketing system was reestablished. And, in the villages and cities, various types of cottage industry began to develop.

For most of the Nicaraguan people this economic system, though certainly not highly developed, was fairly benign. Although he may have been exaggerating slightly, one observer writing in the early 1870s noted that "peonage such as is seen in Mexico and various parts of Spanish America does not exist in Nicaragua. . . . Any citizen whatever can set himself up on a piece of open land . . . to cultivate plantain and corn."[3]

Primitive Dependent Capitalism

The relative isolation of Nicaragua and the gradual development of an internally oriented economy were abruptly interrupted by the coffee boom that hit Central America in the late 1800s. Coffee was probably introduced into the country as an exotic curiosity in the first quarter of the nineteenth century. By 1848 it was being produced commercially on a small scale. In the early 1850s it was a favorite beverage of the twenty thousand or so foreign passengers each month who utilized Cornelius Vanderbilt's Accessory Transit Company route across Nicaragua on their way to California.[4] But it was not until the 1870s that coffee really came into its own. By then the international demand was so strong that the country's ruling elite was motivated to monopolize and redirect much of Nicaragua's productive capacity toward the cultivation of that one export product.

Two factors of crucial importance to the production of coffee are fertile land in the right climatological setting and a large, essentially unskilled work force that can be called upon to offer its services for a few months during the harvest season. In Nicaragua in the early 1870s both were in short supply. The coffee culture had already moved into most of the exploitable lands around Managua, and other promising lands in the northern highlands were occupied by independent peasants and members of Indian communes engaged in traditional subsistence farming. And as the rural masses had access to their own land, there was no pool of vulnerable and easily exploitable peons.

The traditional elite solved both of these problems with ingenuity and speed. In the late 1870s and 1880s they took the land they coveted and created the work force they needed through a combination of chicanery, violence, and self-serving legislation. Individual squatter farmers and Indians working the land through communal arrangements were extremely vulnerable to legal manipulation because, in most cases, these people held rights to the land by tradition rather than by legal title. For several decades the agrarian elite had attempted, through legislation, to abolish communal and squatter landholdings. In 1877, under the presidency of Conservative Pedro Joaquín Chamorro, an agrarian law was passed that outlawed communal holdings and gave individuals the right to buy "unoccupied" national lands. The resulting massive dislocation of Indian communal farmers and individual peasants led inevitably to the War of the Comuneros of 1881 in the Pacific and north-central regions of Nicaragua. After a series of cruel battles in which as many as five thousand Indians may have been killed,[5] the new order was imposed on the region. Coffee was free to expand into new land.

The laws that forced the small farmer off the land also helped create a vulnerable rural proletariat. To reinforce this phenomenon the elite-controlled governments also passed laws against "vagrancy" and the cultivation of plantain — the banana-like staple food of the peasants.[6] Forced to buy staples at high prices in the plantation commissaries, many coffee workers were forced to rely on credit from these company stores. Before long they were trapped into a very effective system of debt peonage. In less than a decade, the self-sufficient peasantry of a large section of the country had been converted into a dependent and oppressed rural proletariat. Most rural Nicaraguans began to lead a life of insecurity, fluctuating between the good times of the coffee harvest, from November through February, and the hardship and unemployment of the *tiempo muerto* (dead period) between harvests.

The growth of the coffee culture also marked the birth of dependent capitalism in Nicaragua. Before this period the economy was based on traditional cattle ranching and subsistence peasant and communal farming. Neither involved a significant use of capital. Coffee, however, was different. First, years before the first harvest, the planter had to make a significant investment in preparing the land and planting and nurturing the seedlings. When the trees began to bear fruit, it was necessary to spend considerable sums of money on manpower and machinery. A large work force was needed for the hand-picking of the coffee berries, and more people and machinery were employed in weighing, pulping, drying, sorting, sacking, and transporting the product.

It is not surprising, then, that although some small farmers converted to coffee bean production, most of those who went into this new enterprise were large landholders, prosperous commercial speculators, and, in some cases, foreigners. The Conservative oligarchy used its control of the legislative process to pass the Subsidy Laws of 1879 and 1889, which gave planters of all nationalities cultivating more than five thousand trees a subsidy of five cents per tree.[7] Among other things, these laws encouraged foreign colonists to seek their fortunes on the fertile slopes of the central highlands. With them came an infusion of new capital.

Once established as the cornerstone of the Nicaraguan economy, coffee held that position until the 1950s. This is not to say that other forms of agriculture were completely wiped out. Some farsighted peasants chose to flee the new coffee zones entirely, moving on to subsistence farming on land in other regions that were not yet coveted by the landed elite. In addition, the traditional precapitalist cattle *hacienda* (ranch) of the lowlands, though now less important, was by no means completely eclipsed. But overall, coffee was clearly the mainstay of the country's economy.

With the growth of the coffee industry, Nicaragua developed what is often loosely referred to as a "banana republic" economy — one based heavily on a single primary export product. Typically, the benefits of the system flowed heavily to a small domestic elite and its foreign trading partners. Taxes on coffee profits, which might have helped redistribute income to the impoverished majority, were virtually nonexistent. The common citizen was an abused instrument of production rather than a benefactor of the system. The Nicaraguan economy also became subject to periodic "booms" and "busts" produced by the fluctuation of the world price of its single product. In good times the economy grew and coffee planters imported luxury goods and machinery, invested money abroad, and educated their children in the United States and Europe. The first of the Somoza dictators received his U.S. education as a result of such a boom. In bad times, such as those following the onset of the 1929 Depression, coffee prices plummeted and the economy stagnated. Planters hunkered down, lived off savings and investments, and imported fewer luxury items and less machinery.

Typical also of the banana republic syndrome was the fact that throughout most of the period little effort was made by the governments of Nicaragua to see that the economy served the purpose of genuine national development. The notable exception to this rule was the regime of Liberal strongman José Santos Zelaya from 1893 to 1909. Zelaya had no real quarrel with laissez faire economics or with coffee. Indeed, he helped the coffee industry by opening up new lands and improving Nicaragua's transportation network. Nevertheless, he also emphasized education, brought fiscal responsibility to the government, created the rudiments of a modern administrative structure, and insisted on national economic self-determination. His refusal to concede to the United States canal rights that would have diminished the economic and political sovereignty of his country and his subsequent negotiation with other powers for a more equitable canal treaty contributed to the U.S. decision to encourage, and then reinforce militarily, the Conservative rebellion of 1909. After Zelaya, the Conservatives, and later the much-chastened Liberals, provided governments whose economic policies fit the banana republic model closely. Within a few years of their ascent to power, the Conservatives gave their U.S. protectors essentially the same canal treaty Zelaya had rejected. From then until the 1950s virtually no effort was made to alter Nicaragua's established role as a provider of a single primary product.

Modern Dependent Capitalism

The quarter century preceding the War of Liberation was a time of economic modernization and dependent "development." New products were added to Nicaragua's portfolio of exports, technology and technocrats became faddish, the government bureaucracy grew rapidly, expanding – at least on paper – into various social service areas, and the gross national product grew in respectable spurts. But the benefits of this change and growth did not "trickle down" to most Nicaraguans. Their perilous standard of living remained essentially constant as the gap between them and the tiny middle and upper classes widened relentlessly.

One of the most obvious changes to occur during this period was the diversification of Nicaragua's exports. In addition to coffee and beef products, Nicaragua now exported significant quantities of cotton, sugar, bananas, wood and seafood. The most important new product was cotton. The sharp increase in the world price of this raw material in the early 1950s, flowing out of heightened demand during the Korean War, motivated Nicaraguan planters and speculators to invest in cotton production in the Pacific lowlands. Nicaragua, which had exported only 379 metric tons of cotton in 1949, increased that figure to 43,971 metric tons in 1955. Eventually as much as 80 percent of the cultivated land on the Pacific coast was converted to cotton.[8] Some cattle ranches became cotton plantations, but, as in the case of the coffee boom seven decades earlier, much of the land that went into the production of this new export product was appropriated in one way or another from peasant producers of grains and domestic staples. Once again independent farmers were transformed into a rootless rural proletariat in the name of "progress" and "development" for the privileged few.

Cotton, like coffee, was subject to cycles of boom and bust. The first period of bust began in 1956, three years after the end of the Korean War. Compared with coffee, cotton was a very capital-intensive activity. It required great investments in machinery, fertilizer, insecticides, and labor. In Nicaragua's case, cotton came to account for almost all of the tractors and harvesters, most of the irrigation systems, and more than three-fourths of the commercial fertilizer used in the country.[9] Small-scale production of cotton was simply out of the question.

Another factor that affected the Nicaraguan economy in this period was the birth of the Alliance for Progress in the early 1960s. A U.S.-sponsored response to the revolutionary success of Fidel Castro in Cuba, the alliance was designed to bring about social and economic development in Latin America through politically moderate means. Enlightened reform from above would, it was hoped, defuse the "threat" of popular revolution from below. The Somozas and the traditional elite of Nicaragua found the idea of the alliance very appealing. Not that they were particularly concerned with its lofty objectives of social and economic justice. Rather, they saw it in more practical terms as a legitimizing device and a source of a variety of economic opportunities. In return for rather painless paper reforms and the creation of a modern social-service bureaucracy, they would receive increased foreign aid and technological assistance and have access to numerous new business opportunities.

Nicaragua in the 1960s was typified by a peculiar type of neopositivism reminiscent of Mexico in the days of Porfirio Diaz. Technology, foreign investment, and "development"—as defined in terms of growth in gross national product—were the new articles of faith. A group of highly trained developmentalists known as the technocrats or, less respectfully, the "miniskirts," were elevated to positions of great responsibility. The heart of their operations was the Banco Central in downtown Managua. There the dictator-president, the head of the "miniskirts" (Francisco "Ché" Láinez, the bank's director), and the cream of Nicaragua's technocratic community met late into the night planning the country's economy as if they were the board of directors of a large corporation. Feasibility studies were ordered, foreign investment was wooed, and joint ventures were embarked upon. Once a year the Banco Central issued an annual report brimming with tables and analyses concerning the national economy. To help train even more business technocrats, Harvard University's School of Business Administration cooperated in the creation of the Central American Institute of Business Administration (INCAE), located in the outskirts of Managua.

A parallel stimulus for capitalist development in Nicaragua, which coincided with the Alliance for Progress, was the birth of the Central American Common Market in 1960. This attempt at regional economic integration provided increased incentive for both incipient industrialization and the diversification of export products. As such it was, for a while, an additional boon to the privileged domestic and international groups who controlled these activities. However, the Soccer War of 1969, between El Salvador and Honduras, brought about the demise of this integrative effort.

The developmentalist optimism of the 1960s proved to be a hollow illusion. Compared with the rest of Latin America, Nicaragua received relatively little foreign investment—perhaps because doing business in that country normally entailed paying off the Somozas in one way or another. Though economic growth did take place, its benefits were concentrated in relatively few hands. The Somozas and their allies simply used their control of the expanded governmental apparatus and the country's new technocratic expertise to increase their own fortunes. Eventually, in the late 1960s and early 1970s, the technocrats themselves were pushed aside as the corrupt and intemperate Anastasio Somoza Debayle replaced skilled administrative personnel with National Guard officers and other cronies to whom he owed rewards for personal loyalty.

The problem of corruption had existed throughout the Somoza period. Anastasio Somoza García had encouraged corruption in his subordinates as a way of isolating them psychologically from the people and thus making them dependent on him. Although the corporate image of the Somoza system improved during the developmentalist years of Luis and the puppets, official corruption continued unabated. In a conversation in 1977, Luis Somoza's close advisor and confidant, Francisco Láinez, the chief of the "miniskirts" during that earlier period, told me an interesting story. One day Luis Somoza, in a pensive mood, asked Láinez to tell him in all frankness what one thing he, Láinez, would do, if he were in Luis's shoes, to bring development to Nicaragua. Láinez thought for a moment and then responded that he would take each of the major categories in the national budget – health, education, etc. – and see to it that *at least half* of that money actually went for the purposes for which it was ostensibly destined. According to Láinez, Luis simply smiled sadly and responded, "You're being unrealistic."[10] This is not to say that, at the highest levels, money was being stolen openly. That would not have been acceptable to Washington – which was footing much of the bill – nor was it necessary, since the Somozas' absolute control of the government gave them the ability to apply a legalistic patina to the flow of public funds. Even after the patent and massive misuse of international relief funds following the 1972 earthquake, the U.S. government, intent on not embarrassing a good ally, was able for several years to produce audits that appeared to refute claims that these funds had been misappropriated.

A final important economic phenomenon of this last prerevolutionary period was the emergence of three preponderantly powerful economic groups each composed of an assortment of influential firms, individuals, and families with financial operations rooted in distinct major banking systems. The function of these groups seems to have been to pool influence, expertise, and financial power in such a way as to give group members an economic advantage over nonmembers. The negative impact on society was that, by reducing competition, they tended to contribute to "a greater inequality of both power and wealth."[11]

The oldest of the groups had its roots in the first half of the twentieth century. Clustered around the Banco de América, this so-called Banamérica Group was originally probably an economic response by

Conservative Granada-based families and firms to the vagaries of doing business in a country dominated by a dictator from the other party. Whatever its early roots, the Banamérica Group burgeoned into a powerful association of interests and firms including sugar, rum, cattle, coffee, export-import businesses, department stores, and supermarkets. Banamérica's international banking ties were with the Wells Fargo Bank and the First National Bank of Boston.

A second group, clustered around the Banco Nicaragüense, emerged in the 1950s and 1960s as an apparent response to the Banamérica Group. With a clearer identification with León and the Liberal tradition, the BANIC Group included coffee and cotton interests, a major beer industry, merchants and commercial enterprises, land development and construction, and lumber, fish, and vegetable oil processing. BANIC's major banking ties were with the Chase Manhattan Bank.

The third important group was that of the Somozas. It consisted of the family's wide holdings in practically every segment of the economy. For several decades its banking needs had been covered by the national banks – first the Banco Nacional and then the Banco Central. These banks frequently extended loans to the Somozas that would not have been available to private citizens and that frequently were never repaid. Though it probably was not necessary, the Somoza group eventually set up its own bank, the Banco Centroamericano.

Interestingly, the Somoza financial empire in prerevolutionary Nicaragua – though vast and impressive – was less clearly recognized as a "group" than were the BANIC and Banamérica networks.[12] This was probably due to the fact that Somoza interests defended themselves not through their group association per se, but rather through the family's direct control of the government and all of its institutions. The founder of the dynasty, Anastasio Somoza García, acquired many of his agrarian properties at the outset of the Second World War by simply taking over the numerous coffee plantations and cattle ranches that the government confiscated from German landholders. In addition he used his unchallengeable coercive power to acquire other prime properties by simply making Mafia-style "offers that couldn't be refused" to the hapless owners. He and his sons also used their control of the government to pass legislation favorable to their agrarian and business interests, to avoid taxes, to award themselves lucrative contracts, and to create obstacles for economic competitors and political adversaries.

Though the Somoza financial empire had the reputation of being poorly and inefficiently run, this was more than compensated for by the tremendous advantage it enjoyed through direct control of government. By the time the dynasty was overthrown the family had accrued a portfolio worth well in excess of $500 million (U.S.) – perhaps as much as one or one-and-a-half billion dollars. The Somozas owned about one-fifth of the nation's arable land and produced export products such as cotton, sugar, coffee, cattle, and bananas. They were involved in the processing of agricultural products. They held vital export-import franchises and had extensive investments in urban real estate. They owned or had controlling interests in two seaports, a maritime line, the national airline, the concrete industry, a paving-block company, construction firms, a metal extruding plant, and various other businesses including Plasmaféresis de Nicaragua, which exported plasma extracted from whole blood purchased from impoverished Nicaraguans. Finally, the Somozas had huge investments outside Nicaragua ranging from real estate and other interests in the United States to agricultural enterprises throughout Central America to textiles in Colombia. Shortly before their overthrow, they even bought controlling interests in *Visión,* the Latin American equivalent of *Newsweek* or *Time* magazines.

The events of the 1970s accentuated the abuses and defects of the Nicaraguan economic system. In the last years of the Somoza dynasty, it had reached a state that, from the point of view of most citizens, was intolerable. For over a century, the country's rich natural resources had been plundered, appropriated, and abused for the benefit of a tiny minority. Millions of Nicaraguans had become economic instruments rather than fulfilled and participating human beings. Public revenues and foreign aid officially destined "to meet basic human needs"[13] had been routinely laundered to end up in the pockets of the ruling family and its allies. The nation's public and private banks had been used first as instruments for the concentration of wealth and finally as conduits for the export of capital as the erstwhile ruling class began to flee into exile. The War of Liberation of 1978–1979 was as much a product of systemic socioeconomic factors as it was an expression of intense political opposition to a particularly venal dictator.

SANDINIST ECONOMIC POLICY

The economic policy and programs of the revolutionary government that took power in July 1979 constituted a radical departure from those of previous regimes. Nicaragua's new political leaders, though varied in their ideological and social backgrounds, were remarkably united in their sense of historic responsibility and their determination to carry out a social revolution rooted in a New Sandinist Economy that, they said, would "make possible *a just, free, and fraternal human life in our fatherland.*"[14] Intensely aware of the tremendous human costs of the old patterns of dependent capitalism, they were determined to fashion an economic system that would not only eradicate past abuses but transfer the "center of attention" from the privileged minority to the exploited "masses." As they felt the changes they envisioned "could not be conceived within the traditional free market framework,"[15] they set out to construct a planned economy, combining both public and private sectors.

Some of the first acts of the new government involved nationalizing large segments of the economy. All of the properties of the Somozas and their accomplices were immediately confiscated, making the people the collective owner of more than 20 percent of the arable land, numerous industrial and commercial enterprises, and thousands of private homes and mansions. In addition, the government nationalized the banking and insurance systems – the latter because it was unable to cope with the needs of a war-ravished country and the former because of the key and unsavory role it had played in the corrupt economic system that had been overthrown. Now these institutions could be converted into instruments of popular national development instead of devices for income concentration.

There was no immediate intention, however, to socialize completely the Nicaraguan economy. Such a move would have been counterproductive, as the public sector already faced a severe shortage of trained manpower due to the inevitable flight into exile of many members of the middle class and the already greatly expanded role of the state. Indeed, it was predicted that in 1980, the public sector's contribution to the GNP would increase from a prerevolutionary level of 15 percent to only a fairly modest 41 percent. In areas such as agriculture and manufacturing, the private sector, in the short run at least, would continue to dominate total output with contributions of 80 percent and 75 percent, respectively.[16]

In contrast to the past, however, private enterprise would no longer be able to operate without contributing significantly to the national well-being. Underutilized productive capacity – especially in the agricultural sector – would be subject to confiscation. The prices of many products would be fixed by the government. Stiff taxes on income and property would be collected. Laws protecting labor would be enforced. And the new Institute of Internal-External Commerce would act as the exclusive agent for the marketing of export products.

The 1981 cotton harvest. The chronic labor shortage at harvest time, aggravated in 1981 by a bumper cotton crop and greater economic security for the agrarian lower classes, necessitated the mobilization of volunteer labor from among a variety of groups, including urban blue- and white-collar workers (*top*) and the Sandinist Popular Army (*bottom*). (Photos by the author)

On the other hand, efforts were also made to reassure the private sector that it had a future in Nicaragua. Loans were made available to help private industry and agriculture recover from the ravages of the war. Whenever tensions mounted between the government and the private sector, there were consultations with the Superior Council of Private Enterprise (COSEP), the nation's major business association. And less than a year after Somoza's overthrow, the government announced the establishment of a *Ley de Amparo* (law of protection) that – in the best tradition of Latin American jurisprudence – gave Nicaraguan citizens the right to seek redress for, and question the legality of, the everyday activities of government. For businessmen and landholders, the *Ley de Amparo* provided protection against the arbitrary confiscation of property – a problem in the months following the FSLN victory – and other acts of revolutionary zeal committed in the name of the government.

Another major objective of the new government was the attainment of national "economic independence"[17] The containment and ultimate elimination of Nicaragua's foreign debt was seen as a basic ingredient in achieving this goal. The country, it was felt, had to extricate itself from the syndrome of international debt peonage. Accordingly, a patient and lengthy but ultimately successful effort was made to renegotiate the enormous debt with which Somoza had saddled Nicaragua. The contracting of new loans was held to a minimum. Instead, funds needed for increased social expenditures and the servicing of the foreign debt were to be raised by maximizing exports, curtailing imports (especially luxury items), and increasing tax revenues. For example, in December 1979, when the government needed money to create labor-intensive public works projects aimed at combatting massive postwar unemployment, it faced the problem not through the expedient of increasing its foreign indebtedness, but rather by placing a heavy tax on the extra month's bonus pay that all employers were obliged to give their employees.

Another tactic identified by the new economic planners as being essential for the achievement of economic independence was the diversification of Nicaragua's international markets. In the past, the country had sold a few consumer industrial products to other Central American Common Market countries and the bulk of its primary product output to the United States, Europe, and Japan. Now, although taking care to retain these markets, an effort was made to cultivate new outlets in nonaligned and socialist countries.

The most important economic goal of the new government, however, was the redistribution of income to provide "an absolute improvement of the standard of living of the poorest sectors."[18] This objective was pursued through a number of approaches including price controls on rents and basic consumer items, labor-intensive programs to create employment, the enforcement and gradual elevation of the minimum wage, and increased government expenditures in health, education, and housing to augment the people's "social salary."

In all, the economic problems that the Nicaraguan Revolution faced in the wake of the successful War of Liberation were enormous. The chances for failure and stagnation were by no means negligible—especially in view of the fact that the openly hostile Reagan administration was likely to engage in a Chile-like program of economic destabilization against Nicaragua.[19] Yet, for the first time in history, Nicaragua's economic affairs were being directed by an honest and well-intentioned group of young people with a dogged determination and burning patriotism forged during the bloody months and years of armed struggle. And, indeed, by late 1980, these new economic planners had made remarkable strides in reactivating the Nicaraguan economy. No doubt important economic mistakes would be made, but there was reason to be hopeful that, at long last, the country's considerable natural and human potential could be significantly redirected for the benefit of the people.

NOTES

1. Ministerio de Planificación, *Programa de Reactivación, Económica en Beneficio del Pueblo* (Managua: Secretaría Nacional de Propaganda y Educación Política del FSLN, 1980), p. 98.

2. Ibid., p. 99.

3. Paul Levy as quoted in Jaime Wheelock Roman, *Imperialism y Dictadura: Crísis de una Formación Social* (Mexico: Siglo Veintiuno Editores, 1975), p. 29.

4. David Richard Radell, *An Historical Geography of Western Nicaragua: The Spheres of Influence of León, Granada, and Managua, 1519–1965* (Ph.D. dissertation, University of California, Berkeley, 1969), p. 188.

5. Wheelock Roman, *Imperialismo y Dictadura*, p. 77.

6. Ibid., p. 71.

7. Radell, *An Historical Geography*, p. 202.

8. Wheelock Roman, *Imperialismo y Dictadura*, pp. 125, 126.

9. Ibid.

10. From a lengthy conversation with Francisco Láinez in his home in Managua during the second week of December 1977.

11. Harry Wallace Strachan, *The Role of the Business Groups in Economic Development: The Case of Nicaragua* (D.B.A. dissertation, Harvard University, 1972), p. 7.

12. Ibid., pp. 16, 17.

13. A favorite expression of U.S. officials during the Carter administration.

14. Ministerio de Planificación, *Programa de Reactivación Económica*, p. 11. The emphasis is in the original.

15. Ibid., p. 114.

16. Ibid., p. 31.

17. Ibid., p. 24.

18. Ibid., p. 98.

19. For a discussion of the emerging Reagan policy on Nicaragua, see Chapter 7. For an excellent example of how the United States accomplishes the destabilization of Third World regimes it opposes, see U.S. Congress, Senate, Staff Report of the Select Committee to Study Governmental Operations with Respect to United States Intelligence, *Covert Action in Chile* (Washington, D.C.: U.S. Government Printing Office, December 18, 1975).

5

Culture and Society

When the outsider travels for the first time in Central America he or she may expect – as I did on my first trip in 1967 – to find five relatively similar little countries. After all, could a handful of contiguous ministates with little geographic extension, tiny populations of a few million each, and a long history of colonial and early postcolonial union be much different from one another? But they could be, and they are. Undoubtedly, the unique character of original native populations, varying climatological influences, and dissimilar patterns of colonization and economic exploitation all had something to do with Central America's variety. Whatever the causes, the individuality of each country is striking indeed. Nicaragua, for instance, is practically as different from the neighbors with which it shares borders (Costa Rica and Honduras) as it is from those with which it does not (Guatemala and El Salvador). The uniqueness lies more in the areas of cultural traits and national character than in social patterns and structures.

CULTURE

Nicaraguan culture is rich and fascinating. In an obvious sense it is part of the wider Hispanic American culture. Like other Latin Americans, most Nicaraguans speak Spanish, are at least nominally Roman Catholic, and place great importance on the family and the defense of personal *dignidad* (dignity). Yet, embedded in this matrix of Hispanic universality are various traits that Nicaragua shares with only a few other countries or exhibits in complete isolation.

Language is an area in which Nicaraguans have their own special qualities. Unlike most other Latin Americans, they rarely, if ever, use the standard *tú* form of informal address. Instead, like the Argentines, a few Colombians, and some peoples on their borders, they address each other with the archaic, nonstandard, informal pronoun *vos* and modify the person of their verbs to fit. Soon after the Sandinist victory, customs officials were busily stamping each incoming passport with an exuberant colloquial greeting that translates: "Nicaragua awaits thee (vos) with the smile of lakes and volcanos and the brilliant and dignifying sun of liberty."

Nicaraguan language is also spicy. One regional song that is practically the functional equivalent of a national anthem ends with the phrase, "Long live León, jodido!" Jodido and forms drawn from the same root (to screw), unacceptable for use in mixed company elsewhere in Latin America, are an almost essential condiment in Nicaraguan speech. People of all classes and both sexes revel in the appropriate use of pungent vocabulary, double entendre, and off-color jokes. Little is off limits to the irreverent tongue of the fun-loving Nicaraguan. In the old days, the Somozas themselves were the brunt of hundreds of jokes. Priests and Americans have always been favorite targets. And since the Sandinist victory, Nicaragua's new leaders have been mercilessly roasted.

Nicaraguan vocabulary also includes a number of words of non-Spanish origin. Place names and forms used for common rustic items such as green peppers, corn, and turkey reflect the lingering influence of Nicaragua's ancient Indian heritage. On the other hand, the many years of U.S. occupation have left their linguistic impression in the form of numerous adopted English words. To use just one example, when I hitchhiked from the Honduran border to Managua in July 1979, I was, as the Nicaraguans put it, going by "ride."

On a more serious plane of verbal expression, Nicaragua has evolved a rich literary tradition. At the turn of the century, a young native poet, Rubén Darío, won international acclaim as the founder of Latin America's first clearly original literary movement, "modernism." To this day, his birthplace is preserved as a national shrine, and poets and writers in Nicaragua are held in particularly high esteem. Darío was followed in the first half of the twentieth century by a number of writers: Santiago Argüello (prose, poetry, and drama); Gustavo Alemán-Bolanos (novels, poetry, and political tracts); and Salomón de la Selva (poetry). More recently, the poet Pablo Antonio Cuadra, who examines the essence of things nica in his famous book El Nicaragüense (The Nicaraguan), distinguished himself as a contributor to the columns of La Prensa and as the editor of the prestigious literary journal El Pez Y La Serpiente (The Fish and the Snake). Pedro Joaquín Chamorro, the martyred editor of La Prensa, also turned his talents to creative literature. Shortly before his assassination in 1978, Chamorro produced a volume of short stories and two novels, Richter 7 (which depicts the decadence of the Somoza system and the tragic erosion of Nicaraguan culture in the period of "reconstruction" following the earthquake of 1972) and *Jesús Marchena* (dealing with, and written in the colloquial language of, the dispossessed rural poor).[1] Another contemporary writer-philosopher, José Coronel Urtecho, emerged from a conservative background to become a highly respected intellectual catalyst for the War of Liberation. Further to the left, the famous priest, Ernesto Cardenal, won international acclaim as a revolutionary poet before joining the FSLN forces in the field and subsequently serving as minister of culture in the revolutionary government. There was little doubt that the postliberation period – so pregnant with conflicting human emotions and expectations – would also give rise to a rich outpouring of literary expression.

Similarly, Nicaraguans have made notable contributions in the fields of art and music. There is a rich indigenous artistic heritage dating back to precolonial times that currently manifests itself in the pottery, leatherwork, woodcarving, embroidered clothing, and other handicrafts available in local public markets. On a more sophisticated plane, the National School of Fine Arts, founded in Managua in the early 1940s, has produced a number of well-known figures including the abstract painter Armando Morales. In the area of music, Nicaragua also has its formal and folk components. The outpouring of popular revolutionary music generated by the War of Liberation was particularly interesting. Pressured by the Carter administration to improve his human rights image by allowing limited freedom of expression, Somoza relaxed his censorship of radio broadcasts slightly in the year before his fall. As a result, some radio stations devoted considerable air time to thinly veiled or openly revolutionary music. In a very real sense, the haunting and inspiring tunes and lyrics of such revolutionary singers and composers as Carlos Mejía Godoy became the background accompaniment of the young people who fought at the barricades.

Nicaraguans also exhibit their cultural uniqueness in their religious ceremonies. Like Catholics throughout Latin America, the inhabitants of each Nicaraguan city and village hold annual festivities honoring patron saints. But unlike the people of any other Latin American country, Nicaraguans have a week-long celebration for the Immaculate Conception of Mary. The festivities of *La Purísima*, which culminate on December 8, far outshadow other holidays, including Christmas. During *La Purísima*, altars to the Virgin are erected or decorated in homes throughout the country and the people of each neighborhood or village, especially the children, go from altar to altar singing songs and reciting prayers. For their piety, they are rewarded with small gifts – usually edible – that normally include a piece of sugar cane. Even in the wake of the War of Liberation – a time of great economic hardship – Nicaraguans of all classes and political persuasions celebrated *La Purísima* with tremendous enthusiasm. Indeed, one of the most moving sights I saw in that period was that of two teenaged war heroes, dressed in FSLN battle fatigues, standing enraptured in front of a tiny home altar – their Belgian automatic rifles temporarily abandoned on the floor like children's playthings.

Another delightful aspect of Nicaraguan culture is the cuisine. Again, there are elements of both the universal and the particular. Like Mexicans and other Central Americans, Nicaraguans eat corn in the form of *tortillas. Tortillas* vary in size, color, and thickness from country to country. In Nicaragua they are large, thin, and made of finely milled white corn. They are often used as an edible utensil in which to wrap barbecued meat, beans, or whatever one happens to be eating. Another absolutely essential item in Nicaraguan cookery is beans. As elsewhere in Latin America – since most people cannot afford the regular consumption of animal protein – beans serve as the main source of protein. The small red bean to which Nicaraguans are particularly addicted is refried with rice to produce a delicious dish called *gallo pinto* (spotted rooster) – a favorite breakfast food of people of all classes. Like many other Latin Americans, *nicas* also enjoy *tamales.* Their *nacatamal,* however, has its own particular character. Wrapped in a pungent leaf from a banana-like plant rather than a corn husk, it consists of corn *masa* (dough), rice, tomatoes, potatoes, chile, cassava root, and often a small piece of meat. Another very typical Nicaraguan dish is *vaho,* which is prepared by slowly steaming salted meat and various vegetables in layers over the same banana-like leaves in a large covered container. In general, Nicaraguan cuisine is well worth trying. Though usually tastefully seasoned, it is seldom hot. For lovers of "hot stuff," however, a bottle or bowl of fine, lip-mummifying *salsa de chile* (chile sauce) is seldom very far away.

No discussion of food would be complete without some mention of drink. The favorite nonalcoholic beverage in Nicaragua is coffee – the best (very good, indeed) coming from the high country around Matagalpa. Like other Latin Americans, Nicaraguans drink their coffee 50-50, with hot milk, at breakfast and black with sugar during the rest of the day. Other typical sweet drinks are made from toasted cacao and green or toasted corn. In the field of alcoholic beverages Nicaragua excels. The typical lightly alcoholic drinks are beer and the more traditional and indigenous *chicha,* made from fermented corn mash. The favorite hard liquor is rum, of which Nicaragua has one of Latin America's very best, *Flor de Caña* (Flower of the Cane).

Nicaraguan custom associated with drinking is also interesting. Like the Spaniards who offer a variety of *tapas* (hors d'oeuvres) with the drinks they serve, Nicaraguan bartenders feel it a matter of honor and pride to serve a delicious *boca* (literally, mouth) with each round. *Bocas* run the gamut from turtle eggs in season to long-armed river shrimp, *conchas negras* (a clamlike creature served raw in its own juices or live with lemon halves), fried pork ribs or rind, *seviche* (raw fish or shrimp cured in lemon and onions), or any other small delicacy. One bar in Granada was famous for offering whole fried chickens with each bottle of rum.

In all, Nicaraguan culture is rich, varied, and unique. Ironically, however, one of the many sins of the Somozas and their accomplices was to ape and promote foreign culture – especially North American – at the expense of that which was authentically *nica*. Not surprisingly, the preservation and strengthening of Nicaraguan culture was a high priority of the FSLN when it seized power. Their determination in this respect was signaled immediately by the creation of the Ministry of Culture, housed, ironically, in one of the deposed dictator's former residences, El Retiro. Literally as the smoke of battle was clearing in late July 1979, this new ministry was already appealing to the FSLN forces by radio to protect and respect objects of artistic and archeological interest found in confiscated private homes and buildings. Such items, the announcement observed, were part of the people's heritage and should be preserved for possible eventual display in national museums. Soon, too, Sandinist television was broadcasting programs devoted to folk music, dance, and art. Later, the ministry organized special popular brigades of culture, which were sent out into the countryside to give performances, catalogue the existence of archeological sites, record contemporary manifestations of regional culture, and discover and promote native performing groups. And in mid-1980, the ministry produced the first issue of a new literary magazine, *Nicaráuac*, featuring a sampling of the works of a number of revolutionary poets. In short, the revolution had made possible a dramatic resurgence of interest in national culture.

SOCIETY

In social conditions and structures, Nicaragua has much more in common with the rest of Latin America than it does in many aspects of culture. This is not particularly surprising, since most social phenomena are at least partly the product of fairly universal economic and political factors. Nicaragua shares with the other Latin American countries the twin legacies of Iberian colonialism and dependent capitalist "development." Throughout Latin America, the human exploitation and rigid social stratification institutionalized during the colonial era were intensified by the income-concentrating tendencies of modern dependent capitalism.

Demographic Conditions

Like most other Latin American countries, Nicaragua has experienced tremendous demographic change in the twentieth century. Population growth rates have soared, the median age has dropped to below fifteen, and there has been a population shift away from the country toward the urban areas.

The population explosion is a fairly recent phenomenon. True, Nicaragua traditionally has had a very high birth rate. High birth rates seem to be a predictable byproduct of poverty—especially in rural societies. Yet until the mid-twentieth century, the country's fertility was very nearly counterbalanced by the high death rate, resulting in only gradual net gains. In this century, however, major advances in medical science have made it fairly easy throughout the world to significantly reduce death by contagious disease, especially among infants and children. Prodded and assisted by international organizations such as the United Nations, even the most socially insensitive regimes such as the Somoza dictatorship were able to introduce new technologies that significantly reduced the death rate. In the 1950s and 1960s this meant that the Nicaraguan population grew at an annual rate approaching 3 percent. To compound the problem the population was becoming younger and, as a result, even more fertile. This in turn pushed the growth rate in the early 1970s to 3.4 percent annually,[2] which meant that, if nothing changed, the population would double every twenty-one years.

The Somoza regime's response to the population trend was to encourage the people to use birth control devices. A family planning program was created in 1967 that, after about a decade, was operating out of approximately seventy clinics. Even so, it is estimated that only about 5 percent of all women of fertile age used birth control devices.[3]

Nevertheless, though the population growth rate had serious long-range implications, Nicaragua was by no means in imminent danger of a Malthusian disaster as it entered the 1980s. It was still a relatively underpopulated country and there were at least two factors that could be expected to help moderate growth trends. First, movement away from abject poverty has tended, historically, to reduce fertility. Therefore, if the determination of the Sandinist government to raise the standard of living of the people meets with success, one can expect the birth rate to drop. Then, too, one can predict that urbanization in Nicaragua will eventually have a moderating effect on fertility as it appears to have had in other Latin American countries such as Colombia, which underwent that phenomenon a decade or so earlier.

Urbanization in Nicaragua, as elsewhere in Latin America, is also a phenomenon of the twentieth century. In 1900, fewer than one in every three Nicaraguans lived in towns and cities of one thousand inhabitants or more. By 1980, however, approximately half were urban dwellers. Since birth rates in the cities are lower than those in the country, the urbanization of Nicaragua appears to have been essentially the product of rural-urban migration. People were leaving the countryside. They were motivated on the one hand by "push" factors such as land concentration, seasonal unemployment, and inhuman rural working conditions. On the other hand, the cities exercised a certain "pull" by offering somewhat better health care and educational opportunities and the illusion of a better standard of living.

Urbanization has had some important effects on Nicaragua. In a very real sense, it made possible the Sandinist Revolution. Decades of government corruption and insensitivity in the face of the miserable condition of many poor urban dwellers throughout the country provided a powerful incentive for the urban insurrection. Without mass urban participation, the small FSLN army in the field would surely have had a much more difficult time in defeating the murderous National Guard. Another effect of urbanization—one with which the revolutionary government has had to come to grips—is the maldistribution of the work force. During its first year in power the government was faced paradoxically with manpower shortages in some rural areas and massive unemployment in the cities. Its long-range plan for dealing with this problem is to entice movement back to the country by providing better rural health care and educational facilities and fostering more humane living and working conditions.

Social Cleavage

By comparison with many other Latin American societies, Nicaragua is relatively integrated. However, measured against an ideal standard, it still had a long way to go when the Sandinists took power in 1979. The most obvious dimensions of cleavage in Nicaraguan society relate to region, ethnic origin, sex, and class. The first three present less serious problems than the last.

Over the last century the problem of regionalism has become steadily less important. The relocation of the national capital to Managua in 1852 and several generations of elite intermarriage have reduced the old rivalry between the colonial cities of León and Granada to a triviality. In addition, the construction of highways and railroads in the twentieth century has tended to integrate other formerly remote areas. Perhaps the greatest single problem of regional integration relates to the much neglected Atlantic department of Zelaya, where large segments of the population still look upon the central government with distrust.

The problem of the Atlantic region is also Nicaragua's major ethnic problem. The inhabitants of sparsely populated Zelaya are culturally and racially distinct, and they have a history of separateness that dates to pre-Columbian times. Unlike the original inhabitants of western Nicaragua, who were largely of Meso-American origin, the pre-Columbian peoples of the eastern coast were descendants of immigrants from South America. Later, during the colonial period, when the region fell under the control of the British, English-speaking black slaves were introduced into the region. As a result of these factors, most of the people of the Atlantic region speak English and/or Indian languages rather than Spanish, are Protestant rather than Catholic, and have a variety of cultural traditions distinct from those of the country's Hispanic majority.

Not surprisingly, the region in which the Sandinist government found the greatest difficulty in implementing its revolutionary programs was the Atlantic coast. This was not for lack of good intentions. Immediately after the liberation, the government affirmed its interest in the welfare of the region. Attractive billboards in Managua enthusiastically proclaimed: "The Atlantic Coast: An Awakening Giant." The Sandinist television network featured Miskito dance groups. The literacy campaign and virtually every government social program had a component especially designed for the Atlantic coast. And Misurasata, an organization of Indians living in that region, was given a seat on the Council of State. The problem, however, was that many costeños (coastal people) simply did not trust the people of western Nicaragua. When the British crown and pirates dominated the coast, local natives allied themselves with those groups against the "Spaniards" – as western Nicaraguans are still known locally. The Somozas used them in disproportionate numbers in the National Guard because of their willingness to fight westerners. Neither Sandino in the 1930s nor the FSLN in the 1970s had much following on the coast. Indeed, many *costeños* still remember and resent the fact that some of Sandino's guerrilla operations in Zelaya disrupted foreign-owned extractive industries in which they had once been employed. In all, it appears that any real solution to the problem of integrating the coast will require considerable time, patience, and human understanding.[4]

The problem of integrating the Atlantic coast affects less than 8 percent of the country's population, but the issue of sexism affects over 50 percent. As elsewhere in Latin America, values and ideas connected with the concept of *machismo* (manliness) have traditionally affected sex roles in Nicaragua. Though things were changing, Nicaragua was still very much a man's world in the 1970s. The woman's place was in her home and strict double standard of sexual behavior applied. On the whole, women received less education and, when employed, earned less money than men. The plight of poor women was especially aggravated by the nature of the Somoza dictatorship and its National Guard. Officers of the guard controlled a flourishing prostitution industry (shut down immediately after the liberation), and soldiers were rarely punished for rape.

Though it would be naive to think that, even in a revolution, sexism could be abolished overnight, it is clear that the national liberation struggle and the revolution greatly advanced the cause of woman's liberation in Nicaragua. The vital part played by women in the War of Liberation caused a healthy reevaluation of sex stereotypes. The Association of Women Confronting the National Problem (AMPRONAC) set up neighborhood committees that helped organize the urban resistance, and many young women fought and died alongside their male counterparts in the FSLN guerrilla army. According to male soldiers with whom I spoke, women – who made up more than 25 percent of the FSLN army – were not camp followers but fully integrated soldiers who shared all of the responsibility of the campaign. They were admired and respected by their male counterparts. The women veterans spoke of warm bonds of respect and love that marked their guerrilla experience.

In postliberation Nicaragua, women continue to play an active and more equal role. They are prominent not only in the new government but also in the Sandinist Popular Army, the Sandinist National Police, and the Sandinist Popular Militias. In addition, AMPRONAC has metamorphosed into a Sandinist organization, the Luisa Amanda Espinosa Association of Nicaraguan Women (AMNLAE), which is represented on the Council of State.

By far the most serious dimension of social cleavage in Nicaragua is that of class. Before the revolution there was a very wide gap in standard of living between the privileged 20 percent of the population and the impoverished 80 percent. As elsewhere in Latin America, the usual European and North American class categories were inadequate to describe the Nicaraguan class structure. The problem lay in the fact that although the bulk of the privileged class could be described as belonging to a "middle group" or "middle sector" by virtue of occupation and standard of living, they were definitely not a distinct "middle class." Rather than having their own set of values and distinct group identification, members of the middle sector tended to ape and identify with the tiny upper class. The real distinguishing factor in Nicaragua was whether or not one worked with one's hands. Quite simply, 80 percent did and 20 percent did not. Since any physical work was viewed as degrading, the privileged minority was accustomed to hiring lower-class individuals at very low pay to cook their meals, care for their children, clean their homes, tend their yards, shine their shoes, and tote their luggage. This was the "natural" order of things. And whereas *la sociedad,* the people of the upper class or high society, often looked down on members of the middle sector, there was much less distance between the two privileged groups than between them and the impoverished majority.

The distance between the masses and the classes was also maintained symbolically. Titles denoting university degrees – doctor, licenciate, engineer, architect, etc. – were taken very seriously in prerevolutionary Nicaragua. Lower-class individuals were expected to use them with the family name or the respectful *don* or *doña* with the given name in addressing their "superiors." And, whereas the privileged minority were accustomed to employ the familiar *vos* form with their inferiors, the latter were expected to respond with the respectful formal *Ud.* This verbal underscoring of class distance even applied in communication between privileged children and their nursemaids. The child was *Ud.* and the servant, *vos.*

Privileged status was also demonstrated in a number of other ways. Membership in a country club or prestigious social organization, the consumption of imported luxury goods, travel abroad, and the affectation of foreign mannerisms all helped distinguish *gente decente* ("decent people") from the masses.

Although the overthrow of the Somozas was a product of the combined efforts of all classes, it was inevitable that, if it were to be a real revolution with meaningful change, there would be class tension and conflict after the liberation. By definition, social revolution involves a reordering of the relationship between classes. Former privileged groups are asked – or obliged – to make sacrifices so that the nation's limited resources can be redirected into the human development of the majority.

In the case of Nicaragua, the revolution affected the former privileged classes negatively in a number of ways. Overnight the use of *don, doña,* and university titles practically disappeared. *Compañero* or its more compact familiar variants, *compa* or *compita,* became the normal form of address regardless of class. Country clubs were confiscated and opened to the public. The importation of luxury goods was curtailed. Many rural and urban properties were seized, and stiff taxes were levied on property, income, and domestic luxury items such as cigarettes and rum.

Many Nicaraguans understood and were able to accommodate themselves to this new reality. The relatively privileged parents of the more than one hundred thousand high school and college students who participated in the literacy crusade of 1980, for instance, demonstrated their willingness to cooperate with the revolution by giving their children the required permission to join the crusade. Many businessmen and landholders responded to government pleas to reactivate the economy by returning their properties to normal production.

But many members of the former privileged classes were a good bit less generous and understanding. Some simply liquidated their assets and fled the country, joining more than ten thousand Somoza followers already exiled in northern Central America and the United States. Others stayed on, grumbling and resisting. Within days of the liberation, for instance, I was asked by a lawyer friend to help get his teenaged children into an English language program in the United States so they, in his words, would not "waste" the months that school would be out during the literacy campaign. Bitter jokes about the revolution and its leaders became standard fare at some gatherings. Rumors of all sorts spread like wildfire in privileged circles (one even claimed that the immediate postwar shortage of beans and medicine was due to the fact that these precious materials were being diverted to Cuba).

More seriously, fearing that Nicaragua was becoming "another Cuba," many landholders and businessmen refused to cooperate in the reconstruction. They began decapitalizing their properties instead of reinvesting in spite of repeated assurances that a responsible private sector would be preserved and very generous government loans and tax incentives would be forthcoming. Several recently founded or reorganized, elite-oriented political parties began issuing shrill statements reflecting the increasing paranoia of the privileged classes. By mid-1980, self-styled counterrevolutionary "armies" began harassing the government from safe sanctuaries in Honduras and elsewhere in northern Central America. Although they posed no real threat to the regime, they did manage to inflict property damage and take innocent lives, including those of seven young literacy campaigners.

The problem of how to handle the privileged classes is a difficult one for the new government. On the one hand, the uncooperative and, in some cases, downright counterrevolutionary behavior of some members of those groups worries and annoys not only the government but also many citizens who have become increasingly bitter and vocal about the "bourgeoisie." On the other hand, the government can ill afford an escalation of conflict and tension with the former privileged classes that might mean the collapse of the private sector and an accelerated exodus of trained personnel. In all, the complex issue of class is easily Nicaragua's most vexing source of internal division.

REVOLUTIONARY SOCIAL PROGRAMS

The most important long-term concern of the Sandinist Revolution was to improve the human condition of the downtrodden majority of the Nicaraguan people. From its founding in 1961 to its final triumph in 1979, the FSLN repeatedly advocated a variety of sweeping social reforms. Immediately after their entry into Managua, therefore, the revolutionaries began to put promises into effect. Ironically, their efforts have been made very difficult by the terrible domestic economic situation and the huge international debt inherited from the departing dictator and his cronies. The government has had very little in public revenues with which to finance social programs and has been forced to ask the working classes to show restraint in making admittedly justifiable wage demands – especially in the public sector.

In spite of these problems, the revolutionaries made impressive progress in the social area during their first year in power. In order to combat unemployment in urban areas, they embarked on a variety of labor-intensive public works projects financed out of a special Fund to Combat Unemployment. The revenues for this fund, as noted earlier, were raised through a tax on the obligatory "thirteenth month" salary that all employers are obliged to pay their employees at Christmas. The privileged minority of wage earners entitled to more than $150

(U.S.) in their extra month's salary were obliged to forgo that part of their bonus in order that thousands of their less fortunate countrymen be employed. The middle sector complained bitterly, but this fund and other monies – some from international sources – allowed the government not only to provide jobs but also to engage in public works projects designed to improve the lives of the people. These included a fifty-square-block children's park in the heart of old Managua, public dance and assembly facilities, a clean and well-constructed public marketplace, simple and hygienic concession stands, covered picnic areas, sidewalks, paved roads in poor neighborhoods, and the reconstruction of war-damaged roads in urban areas.

The new government was also concerned with improving the lives of the rural poor. Immediately after the liberation, the government confiscated the agrarian properties of Somoza and his cohorts – about one-fifth of the nation's cultivable land. During the following year additional confiscations took place for other reasons, bringing public control of the nation's total arable surface to around 25 percent. Since the land in question consisted of large, fairly modern commercial operations, the government decided not to parcelize its land but rather to organize it into state farms and production cooperatives. In this public sector efforts were made to improve lives of the workers by improving real wages and working conditions; providing small health units, schools, and housing projects; and opening rural stores where prices for basic necessities were kept artificially low.

In the bulk of the agricultural sector that remained in private hands, the government worked in behalf of the poor in a number of additional ways. To help the agricultural proletariat working on large private farms, it began strict enforcement of laws governing minimum wages and working conditions and encouraged workers, through their unions, to insist on their rights. In addition, for the first time in history, small producers were given access to substantial amounts of public credit. In the first year over 50 percent of all public loans to the agrarian private sector went to credit and service cooperatives formed by peasants. Small farmers were also helped by strict controls governing water usage and maximum rents for agricultural lands.[5]

In spite of severe economic constraints, the government also began planning and implementing sweeping changes in public policy toward health, housing, and education. Efforts in the area of health were impressive. Even during the insurrection, the FSLN, through its neighborhood Civil Defense Committees (CDCs), had organized health volunteers to deal with the most pressing medical needs of people in the insurgent neighborhoods. Immediately after the liberation, the poorly coordinated, chaotic, clientelistic health care system inherited from Somoza was thoroughly reorganized into one administratively centralized ministry. The overriding philosophy of the new system was to make health care available to everyone – in rural and urban areas alike – and to minimize costs by emphasizing preventative rather than curative care.

Although the budgetary demands created by the need to rebuild war-damaged hospitals and to care for the wounded made it difficult, the preventative and distributive objectives of the new health program were nevertheless pursued with vigor and imagination. As one aspect of the effort to expand health care, the yearly quota of physicians to be produced by the nation's universities was increased tenfold and a program was initiated to train paramedics to provide basic preventative, diagnostic, and first aid services. Almost immediately after the liberation, the government sponsored a massive immunization program against polio and measles. Using internationally donated vaccines and relying on the voluntary cooperation of the Sandinist popular organizations, this vaccination campaign reached approximately 85 percent of the vulnerable population by the end of 1979. Simultaneously, hundreds of oral rehydration centers were set up around the country to administer simple but effective remedies in an effort to reduce infant deaths from diarrheal dehydration. In connection with this program, graphically explicit billboards were erected throughout the country to urge mothers to bring children with diarrhea immediately to these centers. There was also a greatly increased emphasis on hygiene, health education, nutrition, and latrine building. Finally, in the area of health care delivery in general, the Ministry of Health claimed by the end of 1979 that it had increased the number of citizens covered from 30 percent under Somoza to 70 percent after the revolution.[6]

The new government also has been concerned with helping the people secure what the Sandinists viewed as the basic human right to shelter. As in the area of health, the devastation caused by the war accentuated an already bleak situation in housing. The basic philosophy of the new Ministry of Housing and Human Settlements (MINVAH) is both humanitarian and practical. In the practical sense, aware of the inadequacy, waste, and high cost of public housing programs in capitalist and socialist countries alike, the revolutionaries decided not to embark on a massive government program of housing construction. Some government housing was constructed – especially in connection

with agricultural production centers. But the major thrust of new Sandinist policy was to provide legal protection to the renter and
homeowner and to supply infrastructural, technical, and organiza-
tional support for the construction of new housing. Accordingly,
drastic rent reduction and controls were immediately implemented.
Illegal subdivisions, in which wealthy landowners had been selling
small building plots on the installment plan without supplying basic
services, were nationalized. Monthly quotas, paid directly to the
government, are now used to provide water, sewage, and electrical
systems. The government also moved to outlaw urban land speculation and to make available, through the popular organizations,
materials for self-help community housing projects.

Clearly the most ambitious social project implemented by the
Sandinist Revolution in its first year-and-a-half in power was the National Literacy Crusade of 1980. From March to August of that year all
schools were closed as over one hundred thousand young volunteers
dispersed throughout the country in an attempt to bring literacy to the
majority of the population over ten years old who could neither read
nor write. According to official results the illiteracy rate for persons
ten years old and older was reduced in those five months from over 50
percent to less than 13 percent. Though many people hostile to the
revolution claimed that the Sandinists had greatly exaggerated their
achievement, a fair examination of methods, tactics, and resources
reveals that gains in the general neighborhood of those claimed by the
government were at least plausible.

A literacy campaign of the type carried out by Nicaragua in 1980
would have been impossible in most of the prerevolutionary societies
of Latin America. Prohibitively expensive in an unmobilized society,
such a campaign would also have amounted to an administrative and
logistical nightmare of the first magnitude. For the highly mobilized
society of postliberation Nicaragua, however, this crusade was neither
inordinately expensive nor exceptionally difficult to coordinate and
implement. The key to its success was the voluntary participation of
not only the young teachers and their previously illiterate students but
also of various Sandinist popular organizations (described in Chapter
6), which provided free and vitally important logistical support. Their
efforts were also backed by a substantial segment of the Catholic
Church, the private sector, and various other organizations. Under
such circumstances, the government's major function was simply to
plan the campaign, train the literacy volunteers, and provide some
material assistance. Given a target illiterate population (ten years or
over) of under eight hundred thousand, the student-teacher ratio was

The 1980 Literacy Crusade. In March, 75,000 volunteer teachers departed for rural areas (*top*) while 25,000 stayed in the cities, teaching at night in such unlikely locations as the onion stall of a public market (*bottom*). Though the initial and most ambitious phase of the crusade was completed and commemorated with a

celebration in August (*top*), other aspects of this program such as follow-up education for the newly literate and literacy education in English and Miskito (*bottom*) demonstrated the new government's ongoing concern for basic popular education. (Photos courtesy of Ramón Zamora Olivas of the central office of the National Literacy Crusade) very favorable and the time involved was sufficient to teach basic reading and writing skills.[7]

The idea of a literacy crusade had been gestating for some time. The FSLN – and in particular one of its martyred founders, Carlos Fonseca Amador – had often stressed the need for such a campaign. Planning sessions had taken place before the final FSLN victory. After the liberation, Nicaragua's new leaders forged ahead with this ambitious project in spite of dire warnings by learned international authorities that their effort was premature and destined to fail.

The Nicaraguans were blessed in that they could draw selectively upon the experience of several mass literacy campaigns attempted previously in other parts of the world. In the 1920s, the Mexican Revolution made a primitive attempt at a literacy campaign. In mid-century, Paulo Freire developed a methodology that he first attempted to apply in his native Brazil and then, after the military coup of 1964, took with greater success to other Third World countries, including Guinea-Bissau in the mid-1970s. In 1961, Cuba carried out its revolutionary literacy campaign. Not surprisingly, therefore, the Nicaraguan crusade received the enthusiastic assistance of many international experts. Paulo Freire himself was a member of the crusade's national coordinating body, Cuba sent advisors, the United Nations Economic and Social Council (ECOSOC) supplied verbal support and technical advice, and many individuals, including some U.S. citizens, volunteered.

The crusade was planned in stages. Soon after the liberation, the popular organizations (CDS, AMNLAE, etc.) conducted a surprisingly thorough and sophisticated nationwide census to determine the characteristics and problems of the Nicaraguan people, especially in the area of literacy. At the same time a team of literacy experts worked to prepare a twenty-three-lesson literacy primer. The crusade took place in concentric waves. First eighty selected educators took a fifteen-day seminar in literacy training. After testing what they had learned in the field, each member taught another group; then they and the members of the second group taught hundreds of additional educators, bringing the total of literacy trainers to several thousand. At that point all of the trainers were dispersed to various regions of the country to teach the volunteers. Finally, from March to August 1980, more than one hundred thousand volunteers fanned out across the land to teach the illiterates who had been identified by the census.

In 1980, the Year of Literacy, the crusade became the focus of national attention. The imagery employed flowed out of the War of Liberation of the previous year. This second war of liberation was designed not only to free the masses from ignorance and intellectual subjugation, but, equally important, to liberate the largely middle-class volunteers themselves from their prejudices and stereotypes about Nicaragua's impoverished majority. The country was broken into "fronts" corresponding to the six zones of combat during the liberation struggle. Within each front, there were literacy "columns," "squadrons," and individual *brigadistas* (brigadiers). In many cases the *brigadistas* lived and worked during the day with the peasants and workers whom they taught at night.

From the start, the teaching of "political literacy" was also very much a part of the campaign. Paulo Freire's concept of *concientização* ("consciousness-raising") was essential. Key words, phrases, and sentences in each of the lessons were designed to stimulate discussion and a new patriotism, pride in the revolution and its martyrs, and, especially, a sense of the dignity and importance of the individual. The first lesson, for instance, focused on *la revolución*, words of central political importance that, at the same time, contained all of the basic vowels. Predictably, many members of the privileged classes, as well as a number of foreign observers, saw the campaign as little more than a systematic program of Marxist or Communist indoctrination. It is significant, however, that the Catholic church, which would certainly have been a major loser had these charges been correct, was, for the most part, highly supportive of the crusade. Indeed, the director of the crusade was a priest, Father Fernando Cardenal.

In the end, the key to the success of the crusade lay in massive voluntary participation. No one was forced to participate. Indeed, minors were not allowed to join without the permission of their parents. Yet for five months the streets of Managua and other major cities were strangely quiet as a significant segment of the country's urban teenagers and young adults waged Nicaragua's second war of liberation in the countryside. In all, this participation, the logistical support of the church and the Sandinist popular organizations, and money and materials from all over the world ultimately made it possible for the government to coordinate a massive project at a small cost to itself.

The Literacy Crusade of 1980 was not conceived as a one-shot affair. In the latter half of 1980, the effort to end illiteracy among Spanish speakers continued and similar programs in English and Miskito were begun for the people of the Atlantic region. In addition, follow-up adult education for the newly literate was pursued. In itself, however, the initial stage had been a unique experience in Nicaraguan history and one of the most remarkable programs of its kind in the history of the world. On August 23, the conclusion of the campaign was marked with a huge celebration befitting its significance. On that day, a crowd of more than three hundred thousand people— *brigadistas*, friends, relatives, and well-wishers—gathered in Managua's newly completed July 19th Plaza to hear commemorative speeches. Later many of the young people stayed on to dance into the early morning in what was easily the biggest *fiesta* in the country's history. Nicaragua had changed considerably in little more than a year.

NOTES

1. For a review of Chamorro's works and exact bibliographical citation see either Grafton Conliffe and Thomas W. Walker, "The Crucified Nicaragua of Pedro Joaquín Chamorro," *Latin American Research Review*, vol. 13, no. 3 (Fall 1978), pp. 183–188; or Grafton Conliffe and Thomas W. Walker, "The Literary Works of Pedro Joaquín Chamorro," *Caribbean Review*, vol. 7, no. 4 (October-December 1978), pp. 46–50.

2. United Nations, *1978 Statistical Yearbook* (New York: United Nations Publishing, 1979), p. 70.

3. An anonymous informed source.

4. For useful information about this problem, see Philippe Bourgois, "The Problematic or Nicaragua's Indigenous Minorities," in Thomas W. Walker, ed., *Nicaragua in Revolution* (New York: Praeger Publishers, 1981).

5. For a thorough discussion of the government's programs in the agrarian sector, see David Kaimowitz and Joseph Thome, "Nicaragua's Agrarian Reform: The First Year (1979–80)," in Walker, ed., *Nicaragua in Revolution* (New York: Praeger Publishers, 1981).

6. Ricardo Zambrano, health advisor, Ministry of Health, interviewed by the author in Managua on December 6, 1979.

7. Previously illiterate individuals were ultimately reclassified as literate if they were able to pass a basic reading and writing test upon successfully completing all twenty-three lessons in the literacy primer.

6

Government and Politics

A political system is not simply a matter of electoral procedures, constitutions, and governmental structures. Politics also involves the relationship between groups and classes and all other factors that impinge on the character of governmental output. For this reason, a narrow examination of the formal constitutional and structural characteristics of a government – especially in the Third World context – is frequently not only misleading but also essentially an empty intellectual exercise. This is certainly true for Nicaragua, particularly in the period before the FSLN victory in 1979.

THE PREREVOLUTIONARY SYSTEM

If one had been foolish enough to take seriously the constitutional formalities and stated objectives of the Nicaraguan government during the Somoza years, one would surely have come to the mistaken conclusion that Nicaragua was blessed with a modern democratic form of government that was pursuing praiseworthy developmental goals. According to the constitution, there were free elections, separation of powers, and a full gamut of explicitly guaranteed human rights. To insure minority participation, the major opposition party was automatically awarded 40 percent of all seats in the legislature and minority representation on boards of government agencies, judgeships, etc. What is more, there were a variety of public agencies and institutions such as the Central Bank, the National Development Institute, the Nicaraguan Agrarian Institute, the Institute of Internal-External Commerce, and the Social Security Institute, which were ostensibly designed to cope with the problems faced by a modernizing society. The stated policies of the government were also impressive. The major expressed goal was to develop the country through the modernization and diversification of the economy. Accordingly, highly trained technocrats were given important roles in the development process and lofty five-year plans were issued and subsequently endorsed by lists of international agencies.

All of this, of course, was simply a facade. Government and politics, under the Somozas, were "of, by, and for" the privileged few. Democracy was nonexistent, corruption was elaborately institutionalized, and public policy consistently ignored the well-being of the majority of the population.

Nicaragua was a democracy in name only. Although there were constitutional provisions for the separation of power – with a bicameral legislature, an executive, and a judiciary – in reality, all power was concentrated in the hands of the president. The National Guard was the president's private army. His command over the Liberal party – which in turn dominated both houses of the legislature and all government agencies – meant that the president was, in fact, the only decision maker. Mandated minority participation served only to legitimize the system and to co-opt Conservative politicians. There was never any possibility that the opposition would come to power legally since elections were thoroughly rigged. During campaign periods, there was frequent censorship of the press and intimidation of opposition candidates. On election day, there was multiple voting by the pro-Somoza faithful, tampering with the ballot boxes, and, cleverest of all, the use of a translucent secret ballot that, even when folded, could easily be scrutinized by government election officials as it was deposited in the ballot box.

Given the hopelessly undemocratic character of elections under the Somozas, party organization and activity were shallow and essentially without meaning. The two major parties, Liberal and Conservative, were crusty relics of the nineteenth century. The original ideological differences between them had long since faded into insignificance. Both represented the interests of a small privileged minority and, by the middle of the twentieth century, both had been co-opted and emasculated by the Somoza system.

Officially, the Somozas were Liberals and their governments were Liberal administrations. In fact, however, throughout most of the period, the Liberal party was simply a cosmetic appendage to a system that depended on brute military force. One apparent exception occurred in the late 1950s and early 1960s when Luis Somoza – who enjoyed the trappings of democracy and party politics – encouraged the Liberal party to have a life of its own. In that period, new Liberal leaders emerged and there was some hope that they might turn into real presidential prospects. In the late 1960s, after the "election" of the less politically minded Anastasio Somoza Debayle, these hopes were quickly dashed. Independent upstarts left or were drummed out of the party as the dictator began to maneuver to perpetuate himself in power, and the Liberal party lapsed into its more traditional cosmetic role.

The official Conservative opposition played an even less dignified role. If the Liberal party was the neglected wife of the Somoza system, the Conservative party was its kept woman. Since the facade of democracy was so important to the Somozas, it was imperative that there always be an opposition to run against during elections. Enticed by personal bribes and/or lucrative opportunities inherent in mandated minority participation in congress, the judiciary, and government agencies, the leaders of the Conservative party frequently agreed to provide a legitimizing opposition during the rigged elections. Even on those infrequent occasions when the leaders of the Conservative party mustered the dignity to refuse to participate, the dictators were usually able to convince less important Conservatives to carry that party's banner to defeat.

There were a number of microparties during the Somoza period. A few of the more notable were the Independent Liberal party (PLI), composed of Liberals who, from 1944 on, chose to dissociate themselves from the parent party over the issue of Somoza's continuing dominance; the Nicaraguan Social Christian party (PSCN), formed by young Catholic intellectuals in 1957; and the Nicaraguan Socialist party (PSN), which was founded by local Communists in 1944.

One of the more interesting of the microparties was the Social Christian party.[1] Inspired by progressive papal encyclicals, lay Catholic humanism, and Christian Democratic ideas emanating from Europe, this party attempted to take advantage of Luis Somoza's somewhat more open attitude toward competitive political activity. Stressing the importance of platform, ideology, organization, and tactics, the Christian Democrats not only won a significant popular following, but also penetrated the labor movement and came for a while to dominate the national students' organizations. Though many young Christian Democrats freely admitted their admiration for the courage and audacity of FSLN guerrillas, they felt at that time that a peaceful, democratic solution might still be possible. When it became clear in the early 1970s that they were wrong, the more progressive members of the party split from the PSCN to form the Popular Social Christian party (PPSC), which espoused an increasingly revolutionary position.

Mass-interest articulation through legal channels was also a fairly hopeless activity under the Somozas. Peasants and urban labor, for instance, had almost no input into the political system. Ignorant, illiterate, and geographically scattered, the peasantry and rural proletariat were subject to constant abuse by landowners and the National Guard. An agrarian reform program legislated in the early days of the Alliance for Progress had virtually no impact on the misery of the rural poor. From 1964 on, a private Social Christian-oriented organization – the Institute for Human Promotion (INPRHU) – did struggle to organize and raise the consciousness of the peasants, but in the face of government roadblocks, its efforts were largely ineffectual. In the end, clandestine activity proved to be the only viable alternative. In the late 1970s, the FSLN began organizing rural workers and landless peasants in workers' committees. In 1978, these were fused into a national organization – the Rural Workers' Association (ATC). In the following year, as the War of Liberation neared its successful conclusion, ATC-organized peasants made their contribution by digging trenches and felling huge trees across roadways to block troop movements and by maximizing the first post-Somoza harvest through the seizure and immediate cultivation of *Somocista*-owned lands in the newly liberated areas.

The urban worker was only slightly better off than his country cousin. The organized labor movement encompassed a small minority of all workers and was badly fragmented. In 1977, the major union organizations included the Marxist Independent General Confederation of Labor, with 12,000 members; the government-patronized General Confederation of Labor, with 8,000 to 10,000 members; the AFL-CIO-oriented Confederation of Labor Unity, with 7,000 members; and the Social Christian Confederation of Workers of Nicaragua, with 3,000 members. The right to strike, while formally enshrined in law, was so severely restricted that most of the many strikes that took place in the 1960s and 1970s were declared illegal. Collective bargaining was made all but impossible by Article 17 of the *Regulations of Syndical Associations,* which allowed the employer to fire, without explanation, any two leaders of the striking union. In the long run, the only viable option for urban workers, too, was to organize themselves clandestinely – again under FSLN leadership. Significantly, the urban insurrections – which took place almost exclusively in working-class neighborhoods – turned out to be one of the most important ingredients in the overthrow of the dictatorship.

Not surprisingly, given the nearly complete absence of institutionalized popular input into the political system, the Somoza government was virtually oblivious to the interests of the ordinary Nicaraguan citizen. Lofty-sounding social programs – ostensibly concerned with public health, agrarian reform, low-income housing, education, social security, and the like – served mainly as devices to legitimize the system, attract foreign aid, employ the politically faithful, and diversify opportunities for the pilfering of public revenues. Very little of what the government spent actually trickled down to the people. With members of Somoza's family at the head of most government agencies, a large chunk of each agency's assets went directly to satisfy the family's greed. For instance, in the ten years in which he headed the National Institute of Light and Energy, Anastasio Somoza Debayle's uncle, Luis Manuel Debayle, allegedly siphoned off more than $30 million (U.S.). Under the Somozas were layer upon layer of corrupt bureaucrats who were expected and, indeed, encouraged to help themselves. Honesty, a threat to the system, was discouraged.

Often a legalistic patina was applied to these misuses of public revenues. But the end result was that when the FSLN seized power in 1979, it had to cope with acute problems in health, education, housing, and welfare. To add insult to injury, the departing dictator and his

Whispering greed: During a Somocista gala, Anastasio Somoza Debayle (right) shares a confidence with his uncle, Luis "Tio Luz" Manuel Debayle who, during his ten years as head of the national energy agency, is alleged to have misappropriated in excess of US$30 million. (Photographer unknown)

accomplices, who had left barely $3 million (U.S.) in the public cof-
fers, had saddled the new government with a whopping $1.6 billion
(U.S.) foreign debt.[2]

THE NEW POLITICAL ORDER

If the old political system had been "of, by, and for" a tiny
privileged elite, the revolutionary system that replaced it was clearly
based in and oriented toward the interests of the impoverished majority. Whereas democracy under the Somozas meant rigged elections,
the empty rhetoric of corrupt elite-oriented parties, and the suppression of popular political participation, the new political system not
only involved, but actually depended upon, the mobilization and
voluntary participation of hundreds of thousands of ordinary citizens.
Not surprisingly, this seismic change in the orientation of politics and
government in favor of the "have-nots" was alarming to the former
"haves."

The formal institutions of government in revolutionary
Nicaragua came into existence gradually. In June 1979, before the
final victory, representatives of the FSLN in Punta Arenas, Costa Rica,
announced a program of government. It included the naming of a Provisional Junta of National Reconstruction that, after the liberation,
became the Governing Junta of National Reconstruction (JGRN). The
heterogeneous composition of the junta is described in Chapter 3.
Though the two members who represented the privileged sectors
resigned in April 1980 (one because of poor health, the other for
political reasons[3]) they were soon replaced by individuals of the same
social and economic status.

In the first quarter of 1980, the Sandinist directorate and the
junta also finalized the creation of a Council of State. The institution
that came into being on May 4, 1980, was a somewhat larger and functionally stronger body than that which had originally been proposed
by the FSLN at Punta Arenas almost a year before. Instead of being
limited, as originally proposed, to the approval or disapproval of junta
decisions without modification, the council had the right to initiate
and/or modify legislation. In the words of its first president, Commander Bayardo Arce, it had acquired a "colegislative" function.[4] A
more controversial modification was the expansion of the number of
council members from thirty-three to forty-seven — with the additional
members coming from mass-based organizations associated with the
FSLN. Although representatives of the elite-oriented microparties
complained bitterly at what they saw as a betrayal of the original pro-

gram of Punto Arenas, FSLN spokesmen argued that the amplification of the council was fully justified as a reflection of the dramatic growth of the popular organizations after the liberation. The microparties and elite interest groups that represented the social and economic interests of the privileged 20 percent of the population, they asserted, were still adequately if not over-represented.

The administrative structures and functions of government were also radically changed. In some cases, new ministries and institutions were created. In others, old structures were relabled or reorganized, split or fused, to fit the objectives of a new socially revolutionary order. Even in those cases where old institutional labels were retained, the corrupt clientelistic functions of those bodies were replaced by the socially responsive functions they were supposed to have been fulfilling all along.

The new revolutionary administration was faced with an incredibly difficult task. In many cases, the departing *Somocistas* had destroyed administrative files and records out of spite and to eliminate evidence that might have been used against them in future extradition hearings. In addition, the revolutionaries who occupied their offices in late July 1979 had little or no administrative experience. Finally, of course, the Nicaraguan government was heavily indebted and on the verge of bankruptcy.

Nevertheless, the new administration also had a number of compensating assets. First, many of the revolutionaries were university-trained professionals who had originally opposed the old regime, at least in part, out of a deep sense of frustration over the fact that the system had denied them ways of working productively for the real development of their country. In addition, the Sandinist Revolution attracted an influx of very talented administrative and technical personnel from all over the world. These included intellectual exiles from the right-wing dictatorships of other Latin American countries as well as numerous volunteers and government experts from North America, Western Europe, and various socialist countries. Cuba alone sent more than two thousand technicians in areas such as education, health, communications, military organization, and sports.

In addition, the new administrators were working with a sense of enthusiasm and dedication that contrasted dramatically with the attitude of their predecessors. To a large degree, a mood of self-sacrifice had replaced the motivation of personal gain. In the first year of the revolution, the maximum monthly salary of any public official, including ministers and junta members, was frozen at 10,000 *cordobas* — less than $1,000 (U.S.). Although such wages were not competitive with those available in the private sector, many talented young people worked with great dedication in the public sector. Government offices were a buzz of activity and public officials often worked through the lunch hour, late into the night, and on weekends. Even in the Council of State, simple lunches were served *en sitio* to council members and visitors in an effort to conserve time.

The new administration had other advantages. For one, it had immense popular support and could, therefore, drastically cut costs by delegating much of the responsibility of program implementation to mass voluntary organizations. Then, too, the relative honesty of the new bureaucrats meant that, for the first time in the country's history, the money destined for specific social programs was indeed spent on those programs.

The specific content and character of public policy under the new system was largely a result of the day-to-day efforts of the Governing Junta of National Reconstruction, the Council of State, and the various administrative agencies. At the same time, it was fully acknowledged that the broad boundaries of government policy were ultimately set by the nine-member Directorate of the Sandinist Front of National Liberation. The FSLN, after all, had emerged from the War of Liberation with overwhelming political power. Having mobilized the Nicaraguan people for war, the front subsequently kept them mobilized for revolutionary change through a variety of voluntary popular organizations, ranging from neighborhood block committees to functional associations involving women, youth, children, urban labor, and peasants. This gave the FSLN a massive political base that dwarfed into relative insignificance that of the elite-oriented political groupings. And, having defeated Somoza's National Guard, the FSLN enjoyed total control of formal military power in the country. The Sandinist Popular Army, the Sandinist Police, and the Sandinist Popular Militias stood as a guarantee that the revolution would not easily be reversed. Although the leaders of the civilian government were by no means the puppets that some critics of the revolution claimed, they were under a clear obligation to quickly implement effective change on behalf of Nicaragua's underprivileged majority.

Another interesting characteristic of the revolutionary system was the near total lack of personalism. Collective, rather than individual, leadership was stressed. Perhaps this was a logical reaction to four decades of personal dictatorship, or maybe it represented a conscious effort to strike a new "Nicaraguan model" of revolution. Whatever the reason, one of the first decrees of the revolutionary junta explicitly outlawed the rendering of public homage to any living revolutionary leader. The erection of statues and the naming of parks, schools, or housing projects after fallen heroes was encouraged, but to do so for a living hero or public servant was prohibited. In keeping with this concept, the leaders of the revolution—ministers, junta members, and important individuals in the FSLN directorate—took turns making key speeches at important public occasions. No one individual monopolized the limelight.

Groups and Power

The nature of party and interest organizations in revolutionary Nicaragua was very different from that of the Somoza period. The political center of gravity had shifted dramatically from elite-oriented parties and privileged interest organizations to a popularly based political movement, the Sandinist Front of National Liberation, and its massive interest organizations and revolutionary military establishment. While the government permitted and, indeed, guaranteed the associational rights of non-Sandinist political groupings, it encouraged people to participate in the revolution by joining various FSLN-oriented organizations.

The most important of these groupings were the Sandinist armed forces. During the long years of guerrilla warfare and throughout the eighteen-month War of Liberation, the FSLN army was vastly outnumbered and outgunned by Somoza's U.S.-trained and -equipped National Guard. Numbering only a few hundred during the urban uprisings of September 1978, the regular FSLN forces had grown to only a few thousand by the beginning of the Final Offensive of June 1979. It is remarkable that one unit of this tiny force was able to launch the attack on Managua with only "approximately 125 weapons of war [FALs, M-1s, M-16s, Uzis, Galils, and the like] and ten light machine guns and bazookas."[5] The FSLN won the war not because of its military superiority, but because it was convinced of the rightness of its cause and because it enjoyed the support of most Nicaraguans. The combination of a lean but well-trained and dedicated guerrilla army and massive urban insurgency was more than Somoza's corrupt and demoralized army could withstand.

At the time of the victory, the guerrilla army grew precipitously. In the final days of the war, many thousands of urban insurgents "joined" the FSLN army by simply "liberating" weapons and uniforms from the thousands of surrendering guardsmen. This influx of raw, untrained soldiers was both a blessing and a problem. It allowed the new government to provide police and emergency services from the very start. Indeed, as I traveled through Nicaragua in the week follow-

In July of 1979 members of the rebel militias pose for the author at a check-point near the northern town of Condega. The makeshift uniforms and old M-1 weapon were fairly typical of the urban militias.

ing the victory, I was impressed by the organization, efficiency, and very real courtesy of the relatively untrained young people who were performing police and security functions. Yet, there were problems. Whereas most of the veteran members of the FSLN army had been trained not only in military skills but also in the role of the new armed forces and the social mission of the revolution, the new volunteers had not. In the first year after the liberation, therefore, emphasis was placed on weeding out undisciplined riffraff and training the rest to be politically and socially conscious and humane guardians of the revolution. In regular training and in "criticism and self-criticism" sessions held in the evenings, the young men and women[6] of the new armed forces were reminded that, in contrast to the hated National Guard, their role was to act as servants, friends, and protectors of the people.

In 1979 and 1980, the rebel army and urban militias were transformed quickly into an official armed force composed of three major branches: the Sandinist Popular Army (EPS), of around twenty

A seventeen-year-old veteran —hero of the FSLN Army— and a friend pose for the author in November 1979. His Belgian FAL automatic rifle was the favorite weapon of the small regular guerrilla army.

thousand troops; the Sandinist Police (PS), a few thousand lightly armed peace officers who worked primarily in the urban areas; and the Sandinist Popular Militias (MPS), a lightly armed volunteer force of around one hundred thousand civilians who could be called into service in the event of a military emergency. Each of these explicitly Sandinist-armed institutions fell under the direct control of the nine-person Sandinist National Directorate.

A major function of these new politically conscious armed forces was to protect the revolutionary system. After all, the leaders of the revolution knew that most of the handful of social-revolutionary experiments that had taken place in Latin America in the twentieth century had been snuffed out in simple coups d'etat led by essentially nonrevolutionary military establishments (Guatemala, 1954; Bolivia, 1965; Chile, 1973; and Peru, 1975) and that the one revolutionary system that had held power long enough to make real social reforms had been forced to repel a major invasion by a foreign-trained exile army (Cuba, Bay of Pigs, 1961). In addition, the government was understandably nervous about the fact that a major segment of Somoza's National Guard still remained mysteriously intact in Honduras. And it was not particularly comforted that U.S. President-elect Ronald Reagan had campaigned on a platform that "deplored" what it called the "Marxist-Sandinist takeover" in Nicaragua.

The second key component of Sandinist strength was its direct involvement with hundreds of thousands of citizens through various FSLN popular organizations, which the Sandinists had organized in the last years of the Somoza dictatorship and had reorganized and expanded after the liberation. Nicaragua's insurrectionary experience was unique in the history of Latin America. Not even in Cuba in the final struggle against Batista had such a large percentage of the citizenry become mobilized. Nicaragua's massive urban uprisings – complete with paving-block barricade, slit trenches, *fogatas* (tire fires), and communications passageways and tunnels – were unprecedented.

A major key to the front's success in toppling Somoza was its ability to appeal to and effectively organize the people. From the mid-1970s on, laborers were mobilized by the FSLN in their work places through Revolutionary Workers Committees and the Movement of Working People.[7] As early as 1976, the FSLN and Catholic activists had organized peasants into Committees of Agricultural Workers, which in 1978 became the Rural Workers' Association (ATC). In 1977, the front had helped create the Association of Women Confronting the National Problem (AMPRONAC), which agitated for women's rights and protested the wholesale human rights violations of the Somoza regime. In 1978 and 1979, AMPRONAC and the FSLN encouraged the formation of neighborhood Civil Defense Committees (CDCs) whose function, quite simply, was to organize urban neighborhoods and blocks to fight the dictatorship. In the end, the workers' organizations, the CDCs, and some units of the FSLN army organized the urban uprisings while the rest of the guerrilla army, backed by the ATC, handled rural operations.

After the liberation, the FSLN Directorate moved quickly to consolidate the advances already made toward what many Nicaraguans enthusiastically referred to as "popular democracy." A Council of Popular Organizations was created to coordinate and support mass mobilization. Encouraged rather than repressed by the state, the popular organizations expanded so rapidly that by September 1980, an obviously impressed Cuban sports advisor remarked that it had taken Cubans several years to achieve the level of mobilization reached by the Nicaraguan people in one year.[8] Immediately after the liberation, two new associations were created: the 19th of July Sandinist Youth (JS-19) and the Sandinist Children's Association (ANS). The former mobilized young adults and teenagers to participate in activities such as the literacy campaign, and the latter was set up to give poor children – many of whom had actually fought in the war – special group recreational and educational activities. At the same time, AM-PRONAC metamorphosed into a new organization, the Luisa Amanda Espinosa Association of Nicaraguan Women. Named after the first woman to die in combat against Somoza, AMNLAE produced a radio program, published a newspaper, *The Women's Voice*, set up child-care centers, cooperated with the literacy and health campaign, and worked to revamp the legal system of Nicaragua to provide legal equality to women. In addition, the Sandinist workers' and peasants' associations, the Sandinist Workers' Central (CST) and the Rural Workers' Association (ATC) expanded rapidly until, by mid-1980, each claimed membership of more than one hundred thousand.

Of all the popular organizations, however, probably the most important were the neighborhood committees. Created during the war as Civil Defense Committees, these organizations metamorphosed into Sandinist Defense Committees (CDSs). Within a few months, the CDSs had spread out into most of the country. In larger cities such as Managua, they were organized in a pyramidal fashion: groups of fifteen or so block committees elected representatives to zone committees, which fed upward into neighborhood committees, which, in turn, formed zonal committees and, ultimately, one municipal committee. By December 1979, the CDSs had organized thousands of block committees in Managua alone. Even the inhabitants of many privileged neighborhoods initially organized themselves into Sandinist Defense Committees. Eventually, as the inevitable tension between classes mounted, the "bourgeois" CDSs tended to atrophy.

Modeled at least in part on the Cuban Committees for the Defense of the Revolution (CDRs), the CDSs performed several functions of vital importance to any real social revolution. First, they were explicitly designed to guard against counterrevolutionary activity. CDS members were asked to keep an eye on what was going on in their neighborhoods and report anything suspicious. Although this vigilance function was seen by the privileged sectors and some foreign observers as having "ominous," "totalitarian" implications, in fact, reported incidents of CDS abuses of power in this respect during the first year were surprisingly few and trivial. Weighed against the abuses was the pressing need to quash the disruptive activities of renegade national guardsmen and counterrevolutionary paramilitary organizations of both the Right and the Left.

The CDSs also served a very useful function as low-cost program facilitators. They mobilized people at the grassroots level in a wide variety of voluntary activities in support of the government's social programs. They quickly and efficiently distributed international relief food; they helped make possible the nationwide vaccination campaign against measles and polio; they collected bottles for the distribution of badly needed medicines; they played a significant role in the literacy campaign; they carried out neighborhood cleanup drives; they cooperated in an impressive nationwide sports program; and they identified and overcame numerous local problems. Given the grim postliberation condition of the country's economy, the government's determination to extricate itself as soon as possible from old patterns of international indebtedness, and the urgent need, on the other hand, to fulfill a number of potentially expensive social reform promises, the collective, grassroots, voluntary activity organized by the CDSs was extremely important – if not crucial – to the success of the revolution.

Finally, the CDSs and the other popular organizations served the very important function of giving citizens the opportunity to participate in the revolution through grassroots decision making and voluntary activity. A totally new experience for most Nicaraguans, this sort of "popular democracy" provided them with a constructive outlet and meaningful goals at a time when the devastation of war had left a legacy of high unemployment. The popular enthusiasm and energy mobilized by the liberation struggle was channelled into building a new and better society. Participation in such activities gave hundreds of thousands of people a real stake in their revolution.

Though dwarfed by what was going on within the Sandinist movement, non-Sandinist interest and party organizations existed and were relatively free to function in postliberation Nicaragua. Certain groups and parties, though not explicitly Sandinist, were essentially supportive of the revolution; others were clearly alarmed by, and hostile to, the revolutionary project.

In the latter category were interest groups and parties representing the former privileged classes. The major interest association was the Superior Council of Private Enterprise (COSEP), which represented the owners of the bulk of the 60 percent of the economy – agricultural, commercial, and industrial – that had not been nationalized following the liberation. Though functionally represented in both the junta and the Council of State, COSEP was essentially without direct political power. Nevertheless, since the government at that juncture neither wanted to, nor would have been administratively capable of, nationalizing the rest of the economy, COSEP could and did exercise real bargaining power in the political system through the implicit threat of withholding its cooperation in the government's plans for economic recovery. For this reason, high government officials met periodically with representatives of COSEP in an ongoing effort to retain that body's cooperation by assuring it that private enterprise still had a place in Nicaragua.

Closely connected with COSEP and the interests it represented were four microparties: the Social Christian party, the Conservative Democratic party, the Social Democratic party, and the Nicaraguan Democratic Movement. Essentially conservative, and with little popular following, the four used their control of certain commercial radio stations and the country's largest-selling newspaper, *La Prensa*, to criticize revolutionary programs and policies and to press for immediate elections. Though it is unlikely that even collectively they could have attracted more than about 20 percent of the votes, they apparently sensed that early elections might have resulted in directionless populism that would have been less threatening to their class interests.

Other interest groups and parties, though not explicitly Sandinist, tended to support the revolutionary process. Among the pro-revolutionary parties were the Nicaraguan Socialist party (PSN) and the Popular Social Christian party (PPSC). The PPSC, for instance, had split, as noted earlier, with the old Social Christian party to pursue a more revolutionary direction in the early 1970s. After the liberation, many PPSC leaders accepted positions of responsibility in the new government. Most notably, Reinaldo Antonio Téfel became director of the National Social Security Institute.

The Catholic church, though of course not explicitly Sandinist, played a supportive role in the revolution.[9] Before the liberation, the hierarchy first denounced the abuses of the Somoza regime and later called for its overthrow and explicitly condoned the use of violence in achieving that objective. Many priests and nuns worked actively in support of the guerrillas and some even took up arms alongside them. After the liberation, although some elements of the church hierarchy – including the archbishop – displayed some nervousness about the future of the church in a revolutionary Nicaragua, most of the clergy, especially at the lower levels, opted actively to support the revolution. A number of clergymen actually accepted important positions in the government. Most notable among these were Father Miguel d'Escoto, the foreign minister; Father Ernesto Cardenal, the minister of culture; and Father Fernando Cardenal, head of the 1980 Literacy Crusade. As of late 1980, it was clear that most Nicaraguan Catholic clerics had rejected the old argument that people should suffer patiently on earth and be rewarded in heaven and had concluded instead that, since the Bible taught that man was made in the image of God, it was plainly sinful to acquiesce in the exploitation and degradation of the poor.

Political Socialization

There is no society in the world that does not engage in the conscious political socialization of its people. Every society has a set of political values, norms, heroes, and symbols that it passes down – often in a very simplistic form – by means of formal and informal education from one generation to the next. In the United States, children are taught about the American Revolution and the Civil War. They learn the meaning of national holidays. They learn to venerate the memory of Patrick Henry, Benjamin Franklin, George Washington, Thomas Jefferson, and Abraham Lincoln. They are expected, both in school and in voluntary organizations such as the Brownies, Girl Scouts, Cub Scouts, and Boy Scouts, to salute the flag and make the Pledge of Allegiance. In sum, they are socialized to be good U.S. citizens.

If political socialization is important in an affluent and stable society like the United States, it is even more important, indeed crucial, in a country undergoing sweeping social revolution. Therefore, it should come as neither a surprise nor a shock that, after the liberation, the FSLN and the Nicaraguan government placed a heavy emphasis on political socialization. The objective of the revolutionaries was to attack old and inappropriate elite-oriented values that were inculcated under the Somozas and replace them with a revolutionary, egalitarian orientation.

Political socialization in the new Nicaragua took various forms. Soon after the liberation, the names of airports, maritime ports, plazas, neighborhoods, streets, parks, and even sidewalks were changed to honor revolutionary heroes and martyrs, from Zeledón and Sandino to the many young people and children who died at the barricades. Beautiful revolutionary wall murals and billboards ap-

Political socialization in the "New Nicaragua." Following the Liberation, revolutionary values and ideals were promoted through the encouragement of mural art and the erecting of billboards. The mural (*top*) depicts the popular insurrection; the billboard (*bottom*) states proudly "Today the new dawn ceased to be an illusion" (the portraits are of Sandino and Carlos Fonseca Amador, martyred leader and founder of the FSLN). (Photos by the author)

peared throughout the country. New national holidays were created. The 1980 Literacy Crusade had a frank and undisguised political component aimed at raising the social and political consciousness of both the students and the teachers. The popular organizations and the Sandinist armed forces encouraged frequent discussion of the rights and obligations of the "new Nicaraguan." And Sandinist television, radio, and the printed press (*Barricada, Patria Libre,* etc.) all worked to foster a new patriotism and a new set of national values. Although the privileged classes and some foreigners grumbled sullenly about Cuban influence and Soviet communism, one almost never saw a hammer and sickle nor heard any reference to communism. The new revolutionary values were a uniquely Nicaraguan combination of flexible Marxism and progressive Catholicism. Above all, this was an intensely proud, nationalistic revolution.

The Issue of Democracy

After the liberation, the revolutionaries found themselves confronting a very real dilemma. Before their victory, they had criticized the Somoza regime for its nondemocratic character. At Punta Arenas and on other occasions, they had promised to create a democratic system and to hold elections. However, their definition of democracy included social and economic, as well as political, components. In fact, above all, their major interest was in improving the human condition of a majority of their fellow citizens. The formal trappings of elections were simply not enough in and of themselves. In addition, they were well aware of the sad record of formal liberal democracy in promoting social justice elsewhere in Latin America. And, although there was little question that Sandinist candidates would easily sweep any election held in the foreseeable future, it was also clear that elections by their very nature have a tendency to breed personalism, empty promises, and an inclination on the part of public officials to avoid hard decisions that might alienate voters. Furthermore, the Sandinists were well aware of Washington's practice of consciously inflicting economic and, hence, political destabilization on countries that incurred U.S. displeasure.[10] Such destabilization efforts had helped set the mood for the military coups that snuffed out the left-leaning, democratic governments of Brazil in 1964 and Chile in 1973.[11] More recently, the same technique applied in Jamaica had apparently helped create the political environment that led to the defeat of the mildly revolutionary government of Michael Manley in the otherwise "free" election of October 1980. It was obvious that the Sandinists were determined not to let their revolution – won at tremendous material and human cost, including 50,000 dead — lapse into the kind of empty, personalistic populism that had destroyed the programmatic capacity of other Latin American revolutions such as those of Mexico and Bolivia. Nor were they eager to set up a "democratic" system that could subsequently be manipulated from Washington through the destabilization of Nicaragua's still vulnerable and dependent economic system.

The short-term solution for which the Sandinists opted in August 1980 was to declare that elections will be held, but not until 1985. By that time, presumably, the country will have recovered from the war, many of the social and economic programs of the revolution will have been implemented, and the political and social literacy level of the Nicaraguan citizen will have been considerably elevated. Even then, however, the revolutionaries warned, the exact form of political democracy in Nicaragua will be dictated by Nicaraguan reality rather than by the bankrupt models of liberal democracy that have become an off-and-on tradition in other Latin American countries.

NOTES

1. For an examination of the history and activities of this party as of the late 1960s, see Thomas W. Walker, *The Christian Democratic Movement in Nicaragua* (Tucson: University of Arizona Press, 1970).

2. Small wonder that few people in Nicaragua were particularly saddened to hear fourteen months later that Somoza's life of comfortable exile in Paraguay had ended in a crescendo of bazooka and automatic weapon fire. (Though the government of Paraguayan dictator Alfredo Stroessner subsequently captured or killed several Argentine "terrorists" who it claimed were responsible for the killing, circumstantial evidence points to the involvement of high-ranking officers in Stroessner's own military who may have been upset at Somoza's alleged effort to elbow his way into the lucrative drug smuggling business previously dominated by those officers.)

3. Violeta Chamorro had a bad leg and was in a state of extreme exhaustion after the events of the previous two years. Alfonso Robelo's motives for resignation, on the other hand, were clearly political. A wealthy vegetable-oil tycoon, Robelo had a history of political vacillation. Before the liberation, he had helped form the "moderate" Nicaraguan Democratic Movement (MDN) and had warned that an FSLN victory would amount to victory for "totalitarian" communism. Having been appointed to the junta, however, he became, for a short while, an enthusiastic revolutionary and on a visit to Cuba actually praised "the clarity of Comandante Castro's thought." However, early in 1980, he apparently decided that his political future lay with the elite-oriented MDN. Accordingly, he resigned from the junta to begin a bitter series

of denunciations against the government, echoing the fears and interests of the privileged classes. See "Robelo Makes His Bid to Lead the Business Backlash," *Latin American Weekly Report,* May 2, 1980, p. 22.

4. "Afirma el Comandante Bayardo Arce, 'El Consejo de Estado garantiza el Pluralismo Político,'" *Patria Libre,* 4 (Mayo 1980), p. 22.

5. Comandante Carlos Nuñez Tellez, *Un Pueblo en Armas* (Managua: Secretaría Nacional de Propaganda y Educación Política del FSLN, 1980), p. 26.

6. Between 25 and 30 percent of guerrilla combatants during the War of Liberation were women. After the war, although many women joined the Sandinist Police Force and Sandinist Popular Militias, women still composed between 8 and 10 percent of the Sandinist Popular Army.

7. Roger Burbach and Tim Draimin, "Nicaragua's Revolution," *NACLA Report on the Americas,* vol. 14, no. 3 (May-June 1980), p. 5.

8. Raúl Noda, Cuban sports advisor, interviewed by Thomas Walker and Eric Wagner in Managua on September 2, 1980.

9. For an excellent examination of the role of the church in the insurrection and the revolution, see the chapter by Michael Dodson and Tommie Sue Montgomery in Thomas W. Walker, ed., *Nicaragua in Revolution* (New York: Praeger Publishers, 1981).

10. Through its manipulation of international public and private finance, its ability to cut off imports from and U.S. aid to offending countries, and its close relationship with powerful multinational corporations, the United States has had little difficulty in the past in generating economic chaos in target dependent economies.

11. For ample documentation of the successful destabilization of Chile, see U.S., Congress, Senate, Staff Report of the Select Committee to Study Governmental Operations with Respect to United States Intelligence, *Covert Action in Chile* (Washington, D.C.: U.S. Government Printing Office, December 18, 1975).

7

The International Dimension

In November 1979, as I deplaned at Managua's Augusto César Sandino International Airport on my second visit to Nicaragua since the liberation, I stopped to gaze at a large new sign on the main terminal building: "Welcome to Free Nicaragua." For some international visitors, this greeting may have held little significance. For others, it probably reinforced deep-seated fears and suspicions. But for one who had studied and empathized with the plight of the Nicaraguan people for over a decade, this proud salutation was rich with bittersweet meaning. After four-and-a-half centuries of foreign domination and abuse, the Nicaraguan people had finally won the right to proclaim themselves sovereign and independent—a stirring and historic accomplishment. Yet one could not help wondering if it could last. Could a tiny republic of barely 2.5 million people located deep within the geopolitical sphere of influence of one of the world's superpowers actually set an independent course for itself? Even by late 1980, the answer to this question was by no means clear.

NICARAGUA AS A CLIENT STATE

As the reader will probably have gathered from the historical chapters of this book, real sovereignty was almost a totally new experience for Nicaragua. During its first half century of "independence," Nicaragua had been buffeted by the conflicting commercial and geopolitical interests of the United States and Great Britain. In the latter part of the nineteenth century, the modernizing liberal dictator, José Santos Zelaya, had briefly championed the cause of Nicaraguan and Central American self-determination. The British had been dislodged from the Atlantic territories; the cause of Central American unity had been revived; U.S. overtures for a very conces-

105

sionary Nicaraguan canal treaty had been rejected; and an effort had been made to diversify the country's international trade relationship in order to reduce dependence on the United States. However, as we saw, the United States eventually reacted to Zelaya's independent attitude – and especially to the possibility that he might let other international interests build a canal that would compete with the newly constructed U.S. waterway at Panama – by conspiring with Zelaya's Conservative opposition and backing them militarily in their effort to overthrow Zelaya and then to stay in power as a minority party.

During the first third of the twentieth century, Nicaragua's tiny privileged elite – Conservative and Liberal alike – came to realize that its narrow class interests could best be pursued through a subservient, symbiotic relationship with the United States. The Conservatives were the first to get the message. They would never have succeeded in their rebellion against the central government in 1909, nor defeated Benjamín Zeledón's nationalist forces in 1912, had it not been for direct U.S. military intervention. Accordingly, they learned to address their foreign protectors in the most groveling and obsequious manner. For instance, after the defeat of Zeledón, a group of Conservatives of "the highest social, political, and financial standing" sent the local commander of the marines a message of thanks that was clearly tailored to appeal to the ethnocentric and chauvinistic interpretation of Central American reality prevalent in the United States at that time.

> The lamentable situation of these countries, perturbed by constant uprisings, is all the sadder when we consider their proximity to the great American nation, which, founded on wise institutions and inspired by the spirit of liberty and justice, marches at the head of the destiny of humanity. Thus the presence of the American troops among us marks an era of peace for this Republic because she now has spread over us the protecting influence of her altruistic policy.[1]

The Conservative elite also ingratiated itself to the Americans by taking loans with private U.S. banks, allowing the occupiers to run many aspects of the country's public finances, and giving their protectors almost exactly the type of concessionary canal treaty Zelaya had vehemently rejected as injurious to the national interest. Among other things, the Brian-Chamorro Treaty of 1916 allowed the United States to corner the rights to a Nicaraguan canal, thus insuring that the new U.S. waterway through Panama could continue to operate without competition.

By the late 1920s, the Liberal elite also came to realize that its class interests could best be promoted by cultivating a symbiotic relationship with the United States. After the United States blocked one last attempt to remove the Conservatives by force, all of the major Liberal leaders, except Augusto César Sandino, bowed to the inevitable and endorsed the U.S.-sponsored Peace of Tipitapa in May 1927. Having done so, they won the U.S.-sponsored presidential elections of 1928 and 1932.

The behavior of the Liberal and Conservative client governments that nominally ruled Nicaragua during the second U.S. occupation (from 1926 to 1933) was obsequiously pro-American. The occupiers continued to play a key role in the financial affairs of the country. The U.S.-trained, -equipped, and -officered "Nicaraguan" National Guard was rapidly developed and expanded as an immediate response to Sandinist "banditry" and as a long-range answer to the problem of insuring pro-U.S. stability in the region.

One of the clearest examples of the subservient character of these governments can be seen in Nicaragua's docile ratification of the very unfavorable Barcenas Meneses–Esguerra Treaty of 1928. As a result of this treaty, Nicaragua relinquished to Colombia the Providencia and San Andrés islands and certain keys off Nicaragua's Atlantic coast. Though even a cursory glance at a map of the Caribbean would tend to verify Nicaragua's historic right to these territories, Colombia had long maintained a conflicting claim based on rather vague policing authority granted its colonial predecessor by the Spanish crown. While it was certainly not in Nicaragua's interest to relinquish these possessions, the United States benefited in two ways. First, the treaty helped assuage long-simmering Colombian resentment over U.S. connivance and military involvement in the independence of the former Colombian province of Panama in 1903. Then, too, it voided additional Colombian claims that had tended to cloud the validity of certain U.S. rights under the Brian-Chamorro Treaty.

The Role of the Somozas

While it is clear that Nicaragua's status as a client state had developed long before the Somozas took power, it is also true that Anastasio Somoza García and his two sons did much to refine that undignified relationship. Throughout most of the Somoza period, Nicaraguan and U.S. foreign policy were virtually indistinguishable. As a bitter Anastasio Somoza Debayle remarked shortly after his overthrow: "I stood back to back with the U.S. and gave my ally all the support I could muster. . . . [no] president anywhere supported the policies of the United States more devoutly than I did. . . . no such loyalty existed anywhere."[2]

The relationship was one of mutual benefit. The Somozas tailored their foreign policy to the interests of their international protector and the United States, in turn, lavished various favors on its client. Throughout the whole affair, the interested parties whose aspirations and needs were consistently ignored were the citizens of Nicaragua. U.S. personnel occasionally may have experienced some queasiness over the nature of the system they were supporting, but as Franklin Delano Roosevelt is said to have remarked at one point, "Somoza might be an S.O.B., but he is *our* S.O.B."

For their part, the Somozas served the perceived foreign policy interests of the United States in a number of ways. In the United Nations and other international forums, they consistently voted with the United States. They leased military bases to the United States during the Second World War. They allowed Nicaraguan territory to be used as a training and staging area for CIA-sponsored invasions of Guatemala (1954) and Cuba (Bay of Pigs, 1961). They sent Nicaraguan national guardsmen to aid in the U.S. occupation of the Dominican Republic in 1965. And they even offered to send troops to Korea and Vietnam.

In the late 1960s and early 1970s, the last of the Somozas, Anastasio Somoza Debayle, also served U.S. interests as a surrogate enforcer of stability in Central America. In 1964, early in the Alliance for Progress, the Pentagon persuaded the military dictators of Central America to form the Central American Defense Council (CONDECA) to coordinate the enforcement of stability in order, theoretically, that social and economic development could take place. By the late 1960s and early 1970s, the warped nature of dependent economic "development" and the near total absence of beneficial social change led to increased social unrest that, in turn, apparently caused the United States to decide to rely more heavily on brute military control.[3] In these circumstances, Somoza, the dean of Central America's dictators and a rabid anti-Communist, naturally became the principal figure in CONDECA. Under his leadership, joint maneuvers were held, guerrilla foci were located and wiped out, and, for awhile, the status quo was preserved.

Nicaragua, under the Somozas, also served U.S. economic interests. While it is true that U.S. investments in that country were never very significant from the U.S. point of view, it is also a fact that the generally laissez faire economic philosophy of the Somozas strayed little, if at all, from that espoused by the developmentalist economists in the State Department. In more concrete terms, Anastasio Somoza Debayle, in the early 1970s, protected U.S. economic interests at his own country's expense by helping to sabotage Latin American schemes to create coffee and banana cartels for the enforcement of higher commodity prices.

In spite of all this, however, the Somozas were never quite willing to take U.S. "friendship" for granted. They also engaged in an extensive and well-financed propaganda and lobbying campaign in the United States. Millions of dollars were paid to U.S. public relations firms to create a favorable image of their regime among Americans, and full-time professional lobbyists devoted considerable effort to the manipulation of U.S. politicians at all levels.[4] As a result, the Somozas could always count on the fervent support of a large number of U.S. congressmen and senators. Some of these individuals undoubtedly behaved as they did out of honest conviction. However, the subsequent indictment and/or conviction of some prominent members of the so-called Somoza Lobby on charges related to Abscam and other corrupt activities lends credence to long-standing suspicions that more personal and material motivations may have been operative in some cases.

In return for their loyalty, the Somozas received extensive support from the United States. After the beginning of the Alliance for Progress, hundreds of millions of dollars in U.S. loans and grants-in-aid were lavished on Nicaragua, ostensibly to help in various high-sounding social and economic development projects. After the 1972 earthquake, there were additional large infusions of funds destined, supposedly, for relief and reconstruction. In fact, of course, most of the money simply evaporated. Social projects carried out by the Somozas were trivial, most of Managua remained an unreconstructed moonscape, and the positive impact of such economic "development" as did take place fell mainly on the Somozas and a small privileged elite. Yet, since the real purpose of the aid was political rather than social, Washington continued to pour taxpayers' dollars down the Somoza rathole until the day the dictator was finally ousted.

The remarkable inconsistencies in logic underlying the U.S. aid program for Nicaragua were clearly demonstrated in the spring of 1978 when the beleaguered Somoza dictatorship was sent yet another infusion of funds "to meet basic human needs." By that time, the U.S. aid program was so unpopular among most Nicaraguans that a lengthy in-house debate actually took place in the State Department over the questions of whether or not to attempt to send the aid without a public announcement. Finally, it was decided to give the ambassador the go-ahead to announce the aid, as it was felt that, even if secrecy were attempted, someone in Nicaragua would surely leak the information, making the U.S. position even more untenable.[5]

The United States also gave the Nicaraguan National Guard massive assistance, including training, in-country advising, arms, ammunition, and equipment. Indeed, the National Guard was the most heavily U.S.-trained military establishment in Latin America. More members of Somoza's guard had received military training in the United States or at U.S. bases in the Canal Zone than any other military establishment in Latin America,[6] including that of Brazil, a country approximately fifty times larger in population. Virtually all guard officers were U.S.-trained. In reality, then, there was very little that was either "Nicaraguan" or "national" about the Nicaraguan National Guard.

Finally, the United States gave the Somozas considerable political support. With a few exceptions, U.S. ambassadors to Nicaragua were usually individuals of very low professional qualifications who were easily co-opted and manipulated by the family. They tended to act more as agents and cronies of the Somozas than as envoys of the people of the United States to the people of Nicaragua. The two most clear-cut examples are those of Thomas Whelan (1951–1961) and Turner Shelton (1970–1975).

The owner of a grain and potato warehouse and one-time chairman of the Republican party of North Dakota, Whelan received his ambassadorship during the Truman administration shortly after William Langer, chairman of the Senate Judiciary Committee, threatened to block all administration legislation until such time as someone from North Dakota, Langer's home state, received an ambassadorship, a post never before held by a North Dakotan.[7] Although he never learned to speak Spanish, Whelan quickly became an intimate of the Somoza family. When Somoza García was gunned down in 1956, Whelan saw to it that the grave condition of the dictator as he lay dying in a hospital in Panama was not immediately made public. In doing so, he gave Luis and Anastasio time to consolidate their control over Nicaragua. Thereafter, he became a second father to the young Somozas. Years later, a former top advisor to Luis commented nostalgically to me that "He was *our* ambassador."[8]

The case of Turner Shelton is certainly no more uplifting than that of Whelan. An undistinguished, about-to-be-retired foreign service officer, Shelton apparently owed his appointment as ambassador to his friendship with, and campaign contributions to, Richard Nixon. Former consul general to Nassau, he had close ties with Bebe Rebozo and Howard Hughes. Indeed, he later arranged for Hughes to set up residence in Managua. Like Whelan, Shelton spoke no Spanish, but quickly became an intimate friend of the Somozas. It was he who helped arrange the Somoza-Agüero pact of 1971, which enabled Somoza to retain control of the country beyond his original term of office. At the time of the earthquake, when it became apparent that Somoza's personal guard had been thrown into such temporary disarray that it could no longer protect the dictator, Shelton immediately arranged for 600 armed U.S. troops to be flown from the Canal Zone and stationed on the grounds of Somoza's residence to "help in the relief effort." Shelton's incredible callousness to the suffering of the quake victims and his initial reluctance to offer his palatial ambassadorial residence as a temporary site to house embassy operations were so scandalous that Secretary of State Henry Kissinger eventually saw fit to rebuke him. Even so, his ultimate removal from Managua was delayed until 1975, apparently the result of active lobbying by his friend, Anastasio Somoza.

Somoza and Carter

After the overthrow of Somoza, there was a tendency in the United States either to credit or to blame the administration of Jimmy Carter for consciously promoting the downfall of the Somoza system. Such an assertion is unwarranted. It is highly doubtful that the Carter administration ever desired the overthrow of the Somoza system, much less the coming to power of the FSLN. Though the administration's behavior may have contributed to that outcome, the effect was purely unintended.

When it came to office in 1977, the Carter administration was intent on demonstrating that its much-publicized human rights policy could, indeed, find practical application. Unfortunately, the promotion of human rights by the United States was deemed impractical in many parts of the world for strategic and political reasons. However, this was not the case in Nicaragua. There, it was felt that the United States could push human rights without jeopardizing its strategic or economic interests. Unlike some other Latin American dictators, Somoza was sure to follow orders. Since the administration had been assured that the FSLN guerrilla threat had been crushed by Somoza's counteroffensive of the previous two-and-a-half years, it felt that a rights crusade could be implemented without endangering the stability of the system as a whole.

As it turned out, this perception of Nicaraguan reality was badly flawed. Washington was correct in expecting that Somoza would follow orders. In 1977, the administration was successful in getting him to call off the National Guard's campaign of terror against the peasantry and to lift the state of siege and reinstate limited freedom of the press. On the other hand, Washington made two fundamental errors in judgment. First, it underestimated the popularity and resilience of the Sandinist Front of National Liberation. Second, it failed to perceive the fact that an artificial injection of civil and political liberties into a system built on the denial of basic social and economic justice can have a highly destabilizing effect.

The Carter team learned its lesson the hard way. By the end of 1977, it was clear not only that the FSLN had not been wiped out but that it was actually receiving increasingly wide support from important and very vocal civilian groups. Alarmed by this totally unexpected situation, the administration began downplaying its human rights campaign and maneuvering for a peaceful solution that would preserve the National Guard and the old elite while at the same time blocking the FSLN. Accordingly, the human rights report on Nicaragua that the State Department sent to Congress early in 1978 was essentially a whitewash; the administration wanted congressional approval for its economic and military aid packages for that country. In addition, even as the War of Liberation was beginning, U.S. diplomatic personnel were urging Nicaraguans to eschew violence and wait for the next Somoza-run elections in 1981. That summer, at the urging of the National Security Council, Carter even went so far as to send Somoza the infamous congratulatory letter regarding the dictator's promises to improve his performance in the area of human rights. Then came the National Palace operation of August 1978 and the massive urban uprisings the following month. Extremely worried, the administration backed an Organization of American States (OAS) effort at mediation in which an attempt was made to get Somoza and representatives of the privileged elite to agree to a solution that would have removed Somoza, preserved the guard and Somoza's Liberal party, and excluded the broad-based coalition led by the FSLN. Finally, in the summer of 1979, as the FSLN closed in on Managua in its Final Offensive, the United States dropped all pretenses and officially requested the OAS to send a peacekeeping force (a la Dominican Republic, 1965) to Nicaragua. That request, as noted earlier, was unanimously rejected.

In sum, the role of the United States in the downfall of the Somoza system was entirely unwitting. Throughout the process, the most revolutionary outcome ever envisioned by Washington was the creation of what Nicaraguans derisively refer to as *"Somocismo* without Somoza," a political system in which a slightly broader spectrum of traditional privileged elites would have participated in a superficially democratic system under the watchful eye of a cosmetically reorganized National Guard. Not until just before Somoza fell, when it had exhausted all other alternatives, did the Carter administration face reality and begin serious communication with the popularly based Sandinist Front of National Liberation.[9]

REVOLUTIONARY NICARAGUA

In an article written before the Final Offensive and subsequently published in the United States at the time of the FSLN victory, Sergio Ramírez, who was to become a central figure in the new governing junta, made some important statements.

> To think that a new, democratic government in Nicaragua might be hostile to the United States is a perverse fantasy. To think that a new and truly representative Nicaraguan government is going to insist on dignified relations with the more powerful countries. . . . is to think correctly. . . . We aspire to dignity, integrity, and international respect. . . . The United States should learn not to fear the ghosts of its past mistakes.[10]

Immediately after the liberation, both the junta and the directorate of the FSLN made various efforts to convey to U.S. authorities their "wish to develop the best possible relations and to heal the wounds inflicted as a result of Washington's historical complicity with Somoza."[11] These wounds, of course, were raw and painful. The struggle to overthrow a U.S.-backed dictator and to dismantle his U.S.-trained and -equipped army had cost Nicaragua the lives of approximately 50,000 people, or roughly 2 percent of its population. In the United States, that would be equivalent to a loss of 4.5 million people, well over 75 times the U.S. death toll in the entire Vietnam conflict. Nevertheless, given Nicaragua's geopolitical position, its economic dependence on the United States, and the remarkably widespread goodwill of Nicaraguans toward the people of the United States, it was deemed highly important to try to construct good relations with that country. Even in the exuberance of the initial victory, U.S. citizens in Nicaragua were treated courteously. There was no attack on the U.S. Embassy, nor were hostages taken. Normal relations were immediately reinstated and government and FSLN leaders traveled to the United States on goodwill missions. Nicaraguan officials turned out en masse at social affairs held by the U.S. ambassador in Managua. In all, it was hoped "that Nicaraguan-U.S. relations could develop into a model of mutual respect between a revolutionary nation and the dominant power of the western hemisphere."[12]

Although intent on developing good relations with the United States, the new government was equally determined that Nicaragua never again become subservient to any foreign power – East or West. The concepts of self-determination and nonalignment, therefore, became the central principles of Nicaraguan foreign policy. Less than two months after the revolutionary victory, Nicaragua joined the Movement of Non-Aligned Countries. In doing so, the Nicaraguan government expressed its moral solidarity with the people of the Third World. Though they condemned *physical* intervention by one country in another, the Nicaraguans expressed their *moral* support of "poor countries in the just treatment of their national sovereignty and economic independence."[13] Nicaraguan officials frequently spoke out on issues where it was felt that the rights and sovereignty of the people were being violated. This meant that while the new government criticized U.S. assistance to the sanguinary military dictatorship of El Salvador, it also stressed its support for the right of the people of Afghanistan to self-determination.

For many people in the United States, long accustomed to the unquestioning loyalty of the Somozas, this more independent approach to foreign policy was seen as a dangerous drift toward the Communist bloc. The fact that Nicaragua had the audacity to send a sport team to the 1980 Moscow Olympics and saw fit to abstain on two U.S.-sponsored votes in the United Nations for the formal condemnation of the Soviet invasion of Afghanistan was leapt upon as clear evidence of the supposed pro-Soviet leanings of the new Nicaraguan government. In fact, however, the Nicaraguans resented U.S. pressure on both of these issues and, though they disapproved of the Soviet occupation of Afghanistan, they, like the government of India, felt that overwhelming support for the U.S. motion would encourage the United States to expand its military involvement in that region, thus heating up a situation that might otherwise be settled by peaceful negotiations.[14]

In pursuit of the principle of national self-determination and the goal of giving itself greater flexibility in foreign policy, the new government immediately adopted the policy of continuing or establishing diplomatic relations with as many countries as possible – indeed, any country that wished to have relations with Nicaragua and would respect its right to self-determination. This meant that while it quickly reestablished full diplomatic intercourse with the United States and Western Europe, Nicaragua also set up new embassies in Third World and socialist capitals. In Latin America, Nicaragua opened or reopened embassies in practically all of the countries, including Cuba on the revolutionary Left and Brazil, Argentina, El Salvador, and Guatemala on the Right. In the case of the two Chinas, the new government maintained formal relations with Taiwan while, at the same time, developing good commercial ties with the People's Republic. All in all, by the end of the first year Nicaragua enjoyed diplomatic relations with a majority of the countries of the world – over twice as many as under the Somoza dictatorship. In August 1980, one official in the Nicaraguan Foreign Ministry noted with obvious pride that, whereas that ministry had once been a rather small, sleepy operation, it had been necessary to move it after the liberation to a large complex of buildings in order to house the various "area desks" into which it was now organized, much in the style of any modern foreign ministry.[15]

Paralleling the behavior of the government, the FSLN also opened up the equivalent of diplomatic relations with a widely disparate variety of international political movements. In the United States, much was made of the fact that the Sandinist Front established formal relations with the Communist party of the Soviet Union in March 1980. On the other hand, almost no notice was taken when the FSLN opened similar relations with the Permanent Conference of Political Parties of Latin America (COPPPAL), which was sponsored by Mexico's ruling Institutional Revolutionary party (PRI), an organization that almost no one in the 1980s would accuse of being revolutionary in anything but name. Even more significantly, the FSLN also enjoyed a friendly relationship with the Socialist International, an organization composed of the major social democratic parties of the Western world, including the ruling parties of West Germany, Sweden, Austria, and Denmark. Dating to before the liberation, this relationship was cultivated as a central component of the foreign policy of the new government.

Another major goal of the Sandinist Revolution was to reduce Nicaragua's inherited economic dependence and vulnerability. As Sergio Ramírez put it in a speech before the United Nations' Economic Commission for Latin America:

> Unlike . . . somocismo, we want a sovereign national economy which would not be dependent on any system of foreign extortion and subordination and would free us from . . . [our traditional] role as supplier of

raw materials and purchaser of manufactured goods which, over time, obliges us to rely on a system of cyclical and tied financing.[16]

The reduction of economic dependence will not be an easy task. Many factors, some of them mutually contradictory, will have to be taken into consideration. On the one hand, Nicaragua desperately needs international aid. On the other, it can ill afford to accept any but the most concessionary of loan terms. In addition, although it is clearly unreasonable that Nicaragua be asked to repay much of the public foreign debt incurred by Somoza and his accomplices for their personal benefit, it is equally obvious that if an effort is not made to do so, Nicaragua will lose her credit-worthiness in Western financial circles. All of this means that the new Nicaraguan government has been obliged overnight to learn to defend its interests through sophisticated and protracted international economic diplomacy.

The Nicaraguans have been particularly successful in handling the problem of the foreign debt. Early on, they decided to keep their previctory promise to honor the country's financial obligations. However, they obviously were not in a position to pay off a $1.6 billion (U.S.) debt at the interest and on the schedule originally negotiated by the departed dictator. This, and the rather shaky moral position of their creditors, gave them some bargaining power. It was clearly necessary to renegotiate the loans and to obtain concessionary terms. In 1980, the $600 million (U.S.) owed private banks was the subject of long and tough negotiations. The hundred or so creditor banks, represented by a thirteen-bank steering committee, at first insisted on terms that were unacceptable to Nicaragua. Eventually, however, the very real specter of a Nicaraguan default, and the unacceptable precedent it would set, caused the banks to agree to restructure Nicaragua's debt along lines that were described as "unprecedented."[17] These included a twelve-year term, reduced interest, and a five-year grace period.

At the same time, the revolutionary government also has proved very successful in attracting new international economic support while taking care to avoid "a disproportionate growth in the external debt which would only . . . [make Nicaragua] more dependent and less sovereign."[18] By the end of 1980, the Nicaraguan International Reconstruction Fund (FIR) had managed to negotiate over $200 million(U.S.) in low-interest, long-term loans from international agencies such as the Inter-American Development Bank, the World Bank, and the Central American Bank for Economic Integration. Approximately $700 million(U.S.) in additional concessionary loans, grants, credits, and assistance-in-kind had come in from such widely disparate governments as those of Argentina, Brazil, Cuba, Costa Rica, Czechoslovakia, East and West Germany, Mexico, the Netherlands, Panama, Rumania, the Soviet Union, Spain, Sweden, Taiwan, the United States, and Venezuela.

Finally, the long-range objective of economic independence is also being pursued through a policy of diversification of products and markets. The advice of international experts was solicited on the problem of how to diversify Nicaraguan production to make the economy less dependent on fluctuations in the market value of any one product, and the revolutionary government began seeking new international markets so that the country would be less vulnerable to the possibility of economic destabilization orchestrated by one major power.

In spite of these achievements, Nicaragua also has run into several significant international problems. One of these was a tendency on the part of that segment of the international news media based in the United States to paint a rather alarming picture of the Nicaraguan Revolution: "Democracy," as defined in the United States, was not being implemented. Marxists were taking over the country and turning it into a Soviet or Cuban satellite. Many Nicaraguans tended to view this portrayal of their revolution as part of a planned international propaganda campaign. However, it is likely that most of the distortions were due to the basic ethnocentricity of U.S. reporters and the fact that they were producing a product for sale to one of the world's most conservative societies. Whatever the reason, many of the rumors and distorted interpretations that circulated wildly among the disgruntled privileged classes of Nicaragua ended up being published or broadcasted by the U.S. media. In the spring of 1980, for instance, CBS News reported that the Soviet Union had set up a military base in the Nicaraguan city of Estelí.[19] Apparently no one had bothered to take the two-hour trip from Managua to Estelí to verify the rumor. Later, on September 3, NBC aired a ninety-minute program titled "The Castro Connection," which presented an alarmist cold-war interpretation of both the Nicaraguan Revolution and liberation struggles elsewhere in Central America.[20]

Nicaragua also faced problems with several Latin American countries. Not surprisingly, its relations with the military dictatorships in the three Central American countries to the north were frequently strained. The victory of the FSLN had obviously lifted the morale of liberation forces in those countries, most notably of El Salvador and Guatemala. While the Nicaraguans claimed that they were not materially involved, they frequently exercised what they saw as their right to express their solidarity with the oppressed majority in those countries. As a result, many Nicaraguans visiting or passing through those countries were harassed and several were murdered. Relations with Honduras, on the other hand, were made tense by a number of border incidents that often involved armed incursions into Nicaragua by some of the more than three thousand exiled members of Somoza's National Guard who remained ominously and mysteriously encamped in Honduras.

The revolutionary government also experienced a short diplomatic flare-up with Colombia, which arose over the issue of the old Barcenas Meneses–Esguerra Treaty of 1928 in which, as noted earlier, Nicaragua recognized Colombia's claims to certain islands and keys off the Nicaraguan coast. In February 1980, the Nicaraguan government declared the treaty invalid, as it had been signed by a client government during a foreign occupation of Nicaragua. Though it is doubtful that the Nicaraguans really expected Colombia to comply, they asked that Colombia agree to put the issue before the World Court. Colombia, of course, not only indignantly rejected the suggestion but took the opportunity to engage in considerable saber rattling, designed apparently for home consumption. In the end, after both sides had made their points, the issue cooled down and diplomatic relations between the two countries continued on a normal basis.

As of late 1980, the only two Latin American countries that had severed diplomatic relations with revolutionary Nicaragua were Bolivia and Paraguay. The Bolivian government had done so in anger over a Nicaraguan request that the Organization of American States sanction the right-wing military coup that had occurred there in mid-1980. Shortly thereafter Paraguayan dictator Alfredo Stroessner also broke relations when Nicaragua had the audacity to present his government with a petition for the extradition of Anastasio Somoza, who had resided there for most of the period since his overthrow the year before. In all, however, Nicaragua's relations with most of the other Latin American countries were either friendly or at least correct.

The most significant international problem confronting revolutionary Nicaragua has been the relationship with the United States. There, in spite of apparent good intentions on both sides, tension and mutual suspicion have lingered on. For their part, the Nicaraguans have had abundant reason to fear the United States. Their worries in this respect have been based not only on their own sad historical experience but also on their awareness of U.S. behavior vis-à-vis other progressive or socially revolutionary Latin American governments of the last several decades. Would the United States eventually attempt to destabilize their revolution? Would the CIA train a surrogate invasion force? Would marines be landed once again on Nicaraguan soil?

In the United States, on the other hand, Nicaraguan reality is being interpreted not on its own terms, but rather as part of a rapidly rekindling cold war. During the Carter administration, official Washington was divided into two camps. On one side were the president and a substantial segment of the State Department who argued that Nicaragua could be saved from becoming a Cuban or Soviet satellite if the United States extended a friendly hand and gave aid quickly. By giving aid, the argument went, the United States would influence the direction of the revolution and keep it on a moderate course. Opposed to this view were important elements in the CIA, the Pentagon, and the National Security Council that argued that Nicaragua was already beyond saving. The extension of aid would simply waste taxpayers' money and strengthen a hostile regime.

This attitude on the part of the CIA, which surfaced within days of the FSLN victory, apparently stimulated former CIA agent Philip Agee to write an article for *Covert Action* in which he speculated in detail on how he thought the CIA would go about destabilizing and undermining the Nicaraguan Revolution. His article, translated and published in the Nicaraguan daily *La Prensa* in January 1980, apparently served as an important document in the planning of a defensive strategy by the FSLN and the new government.[21]

Meanwhile, President Carter and the State Department proceeded with their policy of rapprochement. Immediately after the liberation, a very substantial quantity of U.S. disaster relief material arrived in Nicaragua and was quickly distributed to needy people through the joint efforts of the Catholic church and the Sandinist Defense Committees. Later, tens of millions of dollars of "pipeline" U.S.-aid funds and loans, originally destined for the Somoza regime, were sent to the new government.

The cornerstone of the new Carter policy, however, was supposed to have been the appropriation of $75 million(U.S.), 60 percent of which was destined to bolster the private sector. Though this bill went before Congress early in 1980, it quickly encountered stiff resistance. Not only was the old "Somoza Lobby" vehemently opposed but, as 1980 was an election year, many Republicans obviously sensed a great opportunity to make political hay at the president's expense. The bill was stalled, amended, and otherwise stonewalled until that fall, when it was finally approved and became law. The congressional battle for this relatively trivial appropriation was one of the most heated fights of its kind in the history of U.S. foreign aid. At one point, the House of Representatives had actually gone into secret session – for the second time in 150 years – to hear classified CIA testimony to the effect that Nicaragua was already "lost." (Apparently the evidence the CIA presented was less than overwhelming, as it obviously did not change many minds.) By the time the $75 million was finally approved, its intended effect in winning the hearts and minds of the Nicaraguan people had been greatly diminished.

However, what really worried many Nicaraguans in 1980 was the attitude of candidate and then President-elect Ronald Reagan and his advisors. The mood was initially set by the Republican party platform of that year, which explicitly "abhorred" the "Marxist-Sandinist takeover" in Nicaragua. In the campaign that followed, it was argued that aid to Nicaragua should be cancelled and that the United States should not deny itself the option of direct military intervention in Central America. "Destabilization" and the rebuilding of exiled elements of Somoza's National Guard for an eventual "Nicaraguan" invasion of that country were also considered.[22]

There was, of course, a good possibility that Ronald Reagan, as president, would act more responsibly than he and his advisors had indicated during the campaign. Simple logic, it was hoped, would show the incoming administration that neither destabilization nor an exile invasion would be sufficient to dislodge the FSLN-created government of Nicaragua. The revolution could count on the support of a dedicated and battle-hardened military establishment as well as that of the vast majority of the Nicaraguan people, hundreds of thousands of whom belonged to the Sandinist popular organizations. And even a massive U.S. invasion, though it might take major urban centers, would only result in a prolonged Vietnam-type war of attrition with a similar outcome. In either event, hostile behavior by the United States would add to the suffering of the Nicaraguan people and almost certainly force the Nicaraguan government, in self-defense, to become authoritarian and to ask for increasing support from the cold war enemies of the United States.

It was also clear that if the United States attempted to undermine the Nicaraguan Revolution, it would do so at considerable international cost. In unanimously rejecting the U.S. proposal that an OAS peacekeeping force be sent to Nicaragua in the final weeks of the War of Liberation, the countries of Latin America had signaled their determination to oppose further U.S. intervention in their internal affairs. By late 1980, the Nicaraguan government was able to create and maintain diplomatic relations with most of the governments of Latin America. Each of the three major powers—Mexico, Venezuela, and Brazil—supported the new Nicaraguan government. Brazil had loaned Nicaragua $30 million(U.S.) for the improvement of its transportation system. Both Mexico and Venezuela had given the revolutionary government various types of aid including concessionary terms for the purchase of oil. Immediately after the November election, Mexico had sent President-elect Reagan a blunt warning to keep U.S. hands off Central America.[23] With their vast oil resources, the Mexicans would obviously be in a position to make their wishes felt.

And there were other important international considerations. As noted above, the world banking community succeeded in negotiating an agreement with Nicaragua for the rescheduling of that country's massive foreign debt. The hundreds of millions of dollars involved in that debt would once again be put in jeopardy if the United States acted in a hostile manner toward Nicaragua. In addition, obviously worried about possible future U.S. behavior, the Socialist International had set up an International Committee for the Defense of the Nicaraguan Revolution, which included an impressive list of leaders of Western Social Democratic parties headed by former West German Chancellor Willy Brandt.[24]

As 1980 drew to a close, Nicaraguans had sound justification for devoting serious attention to matters of defense and the containment of counterrevolutionary activity. At the same time, however, there was good reason to hope that many of the defensive measures being designed would never have to be employed and that the new government could proceed with the task of trying to create a more just and humane society.

NOTES

1. A letter from sixty-one Nicaraguans to Major S. D. Butler, Granada, October 9, 1912. From folder 5 of the "Personal Papers" of Joseph H. Pendleton in the U.S. Marine Corps Historical Center, Washington, D.C., Naval Yard.

2. Anastasio Somoza and Jack Cox, *Nicaragua Betrayed* (Belmont, Mass.: Western Islands, 1980), pp. 77–78.

3. The shift in emphasis can be seen in a report prepared by Nelson Rockefeller after an official fact-finding visit to Latin America in 1969. Nelson A. Rockefeller, *The Rockefeller Report on the Americas* (Chicago: Quadrangle Books, 1969).

4. Though Somoza lobbying efforts were at least as extensive in the 1970s, the most detailed documentation of this type of activity pertains to the early 1960s. U.S. Congress, Senate, Committee on Foreign Relations, *Activities of Nondiplomatic Representatives of Foreign Principals in the United States*, pt. 2, hearing of March 3, 1963 (Washington, D.C.: U.S. Government Printing Office, 1963).

5. From a conversation I had with an informed source in the State Department in April 1978.

6. Richard Millett, *The Guardians of the Dynasty* (Maryknoll, New York:

Orbis Press, 1977), p. 252.

7. See Albert M. Colegrove, "Nicaragua: Another Cuba?" *The Nation* (July 1, 1961), pp. 6–9; and Roland Young, *The American Congress* (New York: Harper, 1958), p. 201.

8. Interview with Pedro Quintanilla, vice-minister of labor and education during the presidency of Luis Somoza, in his home in Managua on July 23, 1967.

9. For an excellent and more detailed examination of U.S. policy during the Sandinist insurrection, see William M. LeoGrande, "The Revolution in Nicaragua," *Foreign Affairs*, vol. 58, no.1 (Fall 1979), pp. 28–50.

10. Sergio Ramírez, "What the *Sandinistas* Want," *Caribbean Review*, vol. 7, no. 3 (Summer 1979), pp. 50, 51.

11. From the manuscript of Alejandro Bendaña, "The Foreign Policy of the Nicaraguan Revolution," in Thomas W. Walker, ed., *Nicaragua in Revolution* (New York: Praeger Publishers, 1981).

12. Ibid.

13. Sergio Ramírez, "Discurso . . . Pronunciado Ante el Plenario de la Comisión Económica Para América Latina (CEPAL), la Tarde de Jueves 27 de Septiembre de 1979, en Nueva York," *Discursos* (Managua: Dirección de Divulgación y Prensa de la Junta de Gobierno de Reconstrucción Nacional, 1979), p. 17.

14. Bendaña, "Foreign Policy."

15. From a lengthy conversation with Carlos Chamorro Coronel, Jefe de Gabinete del Ministro de Relaciones Exteriores, in Managua, August 1980.

16. Ramírez, "Discurso," p. 14.

17. "Nicaragua Makes Peace with Bankers Over Somoza's Unpaid Debts," *Latin American Weekly Report* (September 12, 1980), p. 1.

18. Ramírez, "Discurso," p. 15.

19. "Nicaragua/Council of State," *Latin America Weekly Report* (May 9, 1980), p. 12.

20. NBC "White Paper: The Castro Connection," aired September 3, 1980.

21. Philip Agee, "El Plan de la CIA en Nicaragua," *La Prensa* (2 de enero de 1980), pp. 1, 7.

22. "Reagan's Advisors Step Up Search for the 'Responsible Right,'" *Latin America Weekly Report* (September 26, 1980), pp. 5, 6.

23. "Nicaragua in the Firing Line as the Empire Strikes Back," *Latin America Weekly Report* (November 14, 1980), p. 1. That the Reagan camp had received and was upset about Mexico's stance was clearly indicated in recommendation 1.a. of a leaked in-house transition team report on U.S. policy toward Latin America that called for "a policy for the resolution of . . . political problems with Mexico" and specifically "for handling Mexico's foreign policy vis-à-vis Central America." Pedro A. Sanjuan, "Interim Report on the Bureau on Inter-American Affairs and Related Bureaus and Policy Areas, Department of State" (Washington, D.C.: Office of the President-elect, no date, xerox copy).

24. "Preparing for the Onslaught," *Latin America Weekly Report* (December 5, 1980), p. 10.

SOURCES IN ENGLISH

Aldaraca, Bridget; Baker, Edward; Rodríguez, Ileana; and Zimmerman, Marc, eds. *Nicaragua in Revolution: The Poets Speak/Nicaragua en Revolución: Los Poetas Hablan.* Minneapolis: Marxist Educational Press, 1980.

> A bilingual collection of poems dealing with Nicaraguan history, the insurrectionary struggle, and the victory.

Amnesty International. *The Republic of Nicaragua: An Amnesty International Report Including the Findings of a Mission to Nicaragua, 10–15 May 1976.* London: Amnesty International Publications, 1977.

> Prepared by a respected, London-based human rights watchdog organization, this report did much to draw international attention to human rights violations under Anastasio Somoza Debayle in the mid–1970s.

Bell, Belden, ed. *Nicaragua: An Ally Under Siege.* Washington: Council on American Affairs, 1978.

> A collection of ultraconservative articles designed to demonstrate the need for continuing aid to the Somoza system as the War of Liberation was beginning. The editor later played a role in helping to prepare a "transition team" report for President-elect Reagan on the functioning of the Latin American section of the State Department (cited in Chapter 7, note 23).

Bendaña, Alejandro. "Crisis in Nicaragua." *NACLA Report on the Americas.* November-December 1978.

> Written by a Harvard-educated Nicaraguan sympathetic to the revolutionary cause, this long article is a useful examination of the situation in Nicaragua midway through the War of Liberation.

Booth, John A. *The End and the Beginning: The Nicaraguan Revolution.* Boulder, Colorado: Westview Press, scheduled for 1981.

> Examines the Nicaraguan Revolution from an historical and sociopolitical perspective.

Burbach, Roger, and Draimin, Tim. "Nicaragua's Revolution." *NACLA Report on the Americas.* May-June 1980.

Written less than a year after the liberation, this study provides valuable discussion and analysis of both the war and the new revolutionary system, focusing in particular on the issue of class and revolution.

Camejo, Pedro, and Murphy, Fred, eds. *The Nicaraguan Revolution.* New York: Pathfinder Press, 1979.

Published immediately after the liberation, this short volume contains some useful speeches and interviews, as well as a translation of the new Statute of Rights of Nicaraguans.

Cardenal, Ernesto. *Apocalypse and Other Poems.* New York: New Directions Publishing Corp., 1977.

A rebel priest and well-known poet, Cardenal became minister of culture after the liberation. This volume contains some of his translated poetry.

_____ . *The Gospel in Solentiname.* Two volumes. Maryknoll, New York: Orbis Books, 1976.

Translation of conversations concerning the meaning of the Gospel, which revolutionary poet-priest Ernest Cardenal conducted with his followers in the community of Solentiname.

Cox, Isaac Joslin. *Nicaragua and the United States.* Boston: World Peace Foundation, 1928.

A dated, but nonetheless useful and scholarly, examination of U.S.-Nicaraguan relations in the early twentieth century.

Crawley, Eduardo. *Dictators Never Die: A Portrait of Nicaragua and the Somozas.* New York: St. Martin's Press, 1979.

Of some value simply because it is one of only a few attempts in English to write a short, comprehensive history of Nicaragua. However, this journalistic effort is flawed by occasional factual errors, weak analysis, and the absence of footnoting.

English, Burt H. *Nicaragua, Election Factbook, February 5, 1967.* Washington, D.C.: Institute for the Comparative Study of Political Systems, 1967.

Designed to provide background information for the 1967 "election," this short study does contain some good data about some of the personalities and organizations that played a role in Nicaraguan politics in the mid-1960s.

EPICA Task Force. *Nicaragua: A People's Revolution.* Washington, D.C.: The Ecumenical Program for Interamerican Communication and Action, 1980.

Published early in 1980, this is a solid first effort to systematize and present information about both the insurrection and the new revolutionary system.

Fiallos Oyanguren, Mariano. *The Nicaraguan Political System: The Flow of Demands and the Reactions of the Regime.* Ph.D. dissertation, University of Kansas, 1968.

A scholarly, but somewhat methodologically dated, structural-functional examination of the Somoza system in the mid-1960s. *Note:* This and the other dissertations mentioned in this section are available for purchase in Xerox or microfilm from University Microfilms International, 300 N. Zeeb Road, Ann Arbor, Michigan 48106.

Goldwert, Marvin. *The Constabulary in the Dominican Republic and Nicaragua: Progeny and Legacy of United States Intervention.* Gainesville: University of Florida Press, 1962.

Goldwert's coverage of the Nicaraguan National Guard is briefer and more superficial than that of Millett (1977).

Helms, Mary W. *Asang, Adaptations to Culture Contact in a Miskito Community.* Gainesville: University of Florida Press, 1971.

A solid enthnographic study of a Miskito community in northeastern Nicaragua.

Jonas, Susanne. "Nicaragua." *NACLA's Latin America and Empire Report.* February 1976.

A useful critical examination of the Somoza system and the U.S. role in it since the mid-1970s.

Kamman, William. *A Search for Stability: U.S. Diplomacy Toward Nicaragua, 1925–1933.* Notre Dame: University of Notre Dame, 1968.

A thorough and useful study of an extremely important period in U.S.-Nicaraguan relations.

Lethander, Richard Walter Oscar. *The Economy of Nicaragua.* Ph.D. dissertation, Duke University, 1968.

A substantial but quite traditional examination of the Nicaraguan economic system in the mid-1960s.

Macaulay, Neill. *The Sandino Affair.* Chicago: Quadrangle Books, 1967.

A sound and scholarly study of the guerrilla war led by Augusto C. Sandino against occupying U.S. forces in the late 1920s and early 1930s.

Millett, Richard. *The Death of the Dynasty: The End of Somoza Rule in Nicaragua.* Maryknoll, New York: Orbis Books, tentatively scheduled for late 1981.

An examination of the downfall of the Somoza dynasty focusing on the Somoza government and its relationship with the United States in the last years of the dictatorship.

_____. *The Guardians of the Dynasty: A History of the U.S. Created Guardia Nacional de Nicaragua and the Somoza Family.* Maryknoll, New York: Orbis Books, 1977.

A scholarly historical study of the creation of the National Guard, the rise and reign of the Somozas, and the role played in all of this by the United States.

Nietschmann, Bernard. *Between Land and Water: The Subsistence Ecology of the Miskito Indians, Eastern Nicaragua.* New York: Seminar Press, 1973.

Like the Helms monograph, this is also a very sound study of a Miskito community, the turtle-fishing village of Tasbapauni.

Organization of American States, Inter-American Commission on Human Rights. *Report on the Situation of Human Rights in Nicaragua.* Washington, D.C.: Secretariat General of the Organization of American States, 1978.

One of the apparent motivations for Carter's infamous congratulatory letter of mid-1978 was Somoza's agreement to allow an OAS team to investigate human rights in Nicaragua, *en sitio.* Unfortunately for the dictator, by the time the OAS team arrived in Nicaragua to conduct its investigation, Somoza's National Guard had just finished slaughtering several thousand Nicaraguan citizens after the September 1978 uprisings. This OAS report documents and analyzes Somoza's disregard for human rights in grisly detail.

Radell, David Richard. *An Historical Geography of Western Nicaragua: The Spheres of Influence of León, Granada, and Managua, 1519–1965.* Ph.D. dissertation, University of California, Berkeley, 1969.

A very good historical study of major regions of western Nicaragua.

Rudolph, James D., ed. *Nicaragua: A Country Study.* Washington, D.C.: American University, scheduled for early 1982.

Produced under contract with the U.S. government, this volume will be in the tradition and format of the old Area Handbook series (see Ryan, ed., 1970). Though a new set of coauthors will be involved, it, like its predecessor, will have undergone State Department examination for "political sensitivity" before being published. However, if the reader keeps this fact in mind, he is still likely to find this volume of value for the general information it provides.

Ryan, John Morris, et al. *Area Handbook on Nicaragua.* Washington, D.C.: U.S. Government Printing Office, 1970.

Though written for the U.S. government and concerned in part with "order and internal security" under the Somoza system, this study does contain a great deal of information about a variety of subjects pertaining to Nicaragua.

Selser, Gregorio. *Sandino.* New York: Monthly Review Press, 1981.

A translation by Cedric Belfrage of Selser's excellent two-volume, Spanish-language work, *Sandino, General de hombres libres* (Buenos Aires: Editoral Triangulo, 1958). Contains many of Sandino's writings.

Somoza, Anastasio, and Cox, Jack. *Nicaragua Betrayed.* Belmont, Mass.: Western Islands, 1980.

Somoza's side of the story. Of interest not as a reliable source of information, but rather as an historical curiosity.

Strachan, Harry Wallace. *The Role of Business Groups in Economic Development: The Case of Nicaragua.* D.B.A. dissertation, Harvard University, 1972.

A traditional, but very useful, examination of the major business groups in the Nicaraguan economic system in the late 1960s.

Walker, Thomas W. *The Christian Democratic Movement in Nicaragua.* Tucson: University of Arizona Press, 1970.

This brief study of the Christian Democratic, or Social-Christian, movement in Nicaragua examines party and related interest-group organization and activity during the heyday of the Christian Democratic opposition in the 1960s.

Walker, Thomas W., ed. *Nicaragua in Revolution.* New York: Praeger Publishers, 1981.

A product of the field research of more than twenty scholars, this book systematically examines the Nicaraguan Revolution in its various facets. While several chapters are devoted to the insurrection itself and important international questions, the bulk of this volume is concerned with revolutionary Nicaragua – programs and policies, power and interests.

Index

Abscam, 109

Accessory Transit Company route, 51

Afghanistan, 114

Agee, Philip, 119

Agency for International Development (AID), U.S., 31–32, 34

Agriculture, 2, 9, 49. *See also Huertas;* Nicaragua, agrarian reform in; *individual crops*

Agüero, Fernando, 30, 31. *See also* Somoza-Agüero pact

AID. *See* Agency for International Development

Alemán-Bolanos, Gustavo, 66

Alliance for Progress (1961), 29, 54, 55, 88, 108, 109

Amnesty International, 32

AMNLAE. *See* Luisa Amanda Espinosa Association of Nicaraguan Women

AMPRONAC. *See* Association of Women Confronting the National Problem

Arbenz, Jacobo, 27

Arce, Bayardo, 90

Argentina, 38, 115, 117

Argüello, Santiago, 66

Association of Women Confronting the National Problem (AMPRONAC), 73, 96

ATC. *See* Rural Workers' Association

Austria, 115

Banamérica Group, 56–57

"Banana republic" syndrome, 52–53

Bananas, 16, 54

Banco Central. *See* Central Bank

Banco Centroamericano, 57

Banco de América. *See* Banamérica Group

Banco Nicaragüense, 57

BANIC Group. *See* Banco Nicaragüense

Barcenas Meneses–Esguerra Treaty (1928), 107, 118

Barricada, 41, 102

Beans, 68, 75

Bluefields (Nicaragua), 17, 18

Bocas, 69

Bolivia, 48, 96, 103, 118

Brandt, Willy, 121

Brazil, 47, 82, 102, 110, 115, 117, 120

Brian-Chamorro Treaty (1916), 20, 106, 107

Brigadistas (brigadiers), 83, 84

Broad Opposition Front (FAO), 36, 37

Bunker, El, 36

Butler, Smedley D., 19

Cacao, 68

Cacique (chief), 6

Canal Zone, 110, 111

Capitalism, 47–48

Cardenal, Father Ernesto, 41, 67, 83, 100

129